INDIAN WRITING in ENGLISH

PERSPECTIVES

INDIAN WRITING in ENGLISH

PERSPECTIVES

Edited by

JOYA CHAKRAVARTY

Published by
ATLANTIC PUBLISHERS AND DISTRIBUTORS
B-2, Vishal Enclave, Opp. Rajouri Garden, New Delhi-27
Phones : 5413460, 5429987, 5466842

Sales Office
4215/1, Ansari Road, Darya Ganj, New Delhi-02
Phones : 3273880, 3285873, 3280451
Fax : 91-11-3285873
web : www.atlanticbooks.com
e-mail : info@atlanticbooks.com

ISBN 81-7156-992-7

Typeset at
APD Computer Graphics, Delhi

Printed in India at
Nice Printing Press, Delhi

PREFACE

Indian Writing in English has gained worldwide acceptance and recognition. The emergence of new talent has brought in its wake newer themes, ideas and forms of writing. A number of critical books on Indian Writing in English focus on these aspects. Yet there is scope for further analysis and interpretation. The works of the writers analysed in this edition cover the period from 1947 to 2001.

Let us look at the socio-economic scenario of India after 1947. Independence brought in its wake partition, a traumatic experience, the aftermath of which continues to haunt us even today. Independent India strove to build up her economy. The Indian Government decided to go in for industrialisation. This brought about a great change as agricultural India gave way to Industrial India. Along with industrial development came a host of new problems. Industrialisation led to unprecedented and violent uprootings and migrations of people from villages to the cities. Economic necessity tore up whole communities and sent them on a long forced march in search of livelihood. Evicted from familiar farms and fields, workers in the cities were forced to seek shelter in slums and temporary settlements. This resulted in a cultural and emotional rootlessness. Changes in society find reflection in the works of the writers analysed here. The social commitment of writers and artists cannot be understood without knowing the socio-economic and political circumstances of their times. No work of art can stand in isolation of the empirical reality of its own time. The social compulsions of each period can dictate meanings for the texts.

Independence brought with it displacement and disillusionment. The post-colonial writers had to re-interpret and re-write various issues from a post-colonial perspective. Colonialism had given security—one inhabited a fixed world.

The post-colonial world was a new world—not firm, the ground seemed to be moving. The continued imposition of alien political, economic and social philosophies could not resolve the problems of young India. The writers dwelt on human relationships. Our lives revolve around them in some form or the other. Relationships cannot grow from nothing. They develop through associations and require a long gestation period.

Moreover, a number of Indo-Anglican writers deal with the family as their subject. The family as a social unit is dying in the West, particularly in Great Britain and the United States of America. But in India it still makes a wonderful subject for novels. It is to be remembered, however, that the perpetuation of all societies depends upon the transmission of values through generations. These values are regulated, interpreted and re-interpreted from time to time. This is why the family has been the recurring theme of nearly all Indian writers writing in English.

From the 1960s onwards Indian writings in English witnessed great changes. Writers like Kamala Das, Nissim Ezekiel, Keki Daruwalla and others began to write in a frank and candid manner. The writers noticed a gradual erosion of social values and this is reflected in the literature of this period. No writer could stand in isolation and watch the changes taking place in India. The writings reflect the yearnings, frustrations and desperate anguish of the people. Independence had infused enthusiasm in the people. As the euphoria of independence dissipated, reality with its myriad problems loomed large. Indian English novels reflected this change. The defiant, individualistic protagonists arouse our interest and stir our imagination. Sometimes, some of these novels disturb our established pattern of thought and shock our sensibilities (see *Starry Nights* by Shobha De).

After the 1980s, one finds a definite change in the expression of the Indian Writers writing in English. They have begun to use language in a very effective way. Be it Shobha De, Upmanyu Chatterjee, Mukul Kesavan, Arundhati Roy or Imtiaz Dhakar, one notices how consumerism has taken a firm grip on the life-styles of urban Indians. Material pursuits reign supreme, and this is reflected in the writings of the novelists. Their writings evoke a pictorial image of Indian society and reflect the cultural diversity of India. Writing from the perspective of the fragmented, marginalized, racially discriminated people, the modern Indian English Writers begin to question the imposition of social practices, which are arbitrary. The multi-culturalism of India highlights the cultural differences of the people. There were and are even today elite cultures, subaltern cultures and regional cultures. New writers began experimenting with the form and literary works associated with post-colonial experiences of migration, identity crisis and diaspora began to be written.

Shorn of the security of joint families (see Upmanyu Chatterjee's *The Last Burden*), the Indian urban males and females are learning the tricks of survival rapidly. Television and internet are fast accelerating the loss of innocence that now comes a trifle too early. Information technology has changed mindsets and opened new visions of a world of free communication and interaction. One can seek and obtain information through the internet on virtually anything under the Sun. "Due to commercialism and consumerism, the I-Me-Mine syndrome seeps into the homefronts resulting in heartbreaks, discord, separations and broken households." Interpersonal relationships are undergoing cataclysmic changes and this is reflected in the Indian English novels.

This volume, I am sure, will be of great use to scholars of Indian Writing in English. The contributors have put forth their views and these provide a fresh analysis of the novels. I thank all contributors who responded to my request to contribute articles for this volume. I thank Dr. K.R. Gupta, Managing Director of M/s Atlantic Publishers and Distributors, New Delhi, who has taken great trouble to bring out this volume.

JOYA CHAKRAVARTY

CONTENTS

1

CHAMAN NAHAL'S *AZADI*: AN APPRAISAL

S.C. SINGH

Chaman Nahal, like Khushwant Singh and Salman Rushdie, is a political novelist. *Azadi (1975)*, the best known of his novels, received Sahitya Akadami Award in 1977. Some of his other popular works are *My True Faces (1973), In Another Dawn (1977), The English Queens (1979) and The Crown and the Loincloth (1981)*. The last novel has received wide acclaim, especially in the Russia where the Russian translated edition of 100,000 copies has been released recently.

Nahal has a broad-based historic sense in that he gives a sufficiently wide canvas of the period that he deals with in his novels. In *Azadi*, the period is about seven months, starting with the announcement of June 03, 1947, about the partition of India, till, January 30, 1948, the black day when Gandhi was shot dead. In this brief appraisal, the focus is to analyse *Azadi* as a political novel with the main stress on the novelist's genuine concern for human values and human beings.

The political novel in Indian writing in English has flourished numerically but its intrinsic artistic achievements have been very few. Khushwant Singh, Salman Rushdie and Chaman Nahal are the front rank writers of political novel in the recent times. They reveal in their novels their preoccupations with the cultural heritage of India and they handle events of national significance very effectively. Nahal has amply and adequately illustrated this point of view in *Azadi*.

Nahal, while writing *Azadi*, strongly felt that the partition of

India was unfortunate, politically motivated and full of forced exile. Recalling elsewhere those desperate days, he wrote:

> "[...]. I had been personally exposed to Gandhiji during the last few months of his life. After 1947, he made Birla House in New Delhi his home. Our family by then had migrated from Pakistan to Delhi,[1] and it was possible for me to attend Gandhi's prayer meetings on most evenings. And what caught my eyes was the immense humility of the man. Many of us amongst his listeners were angry young men who had lost everything in Pakistan, including the dear ones who were assassinated in the riots. And we asked Gandhi angry questions. To which he never gave an answer without making us feel that our pain was his pain too. I also saw how plain and ordinary Gandhi was to look at: short-statured, thin, with rather common features."[2]

This shows that the novelist was not happy with the partition of India and he poignantly expressed the feelings of anguish and anger about it in *Azadi* which is predominantly a political novel. The novel opens with the following lines:

> "It was the third of June, 1947. This evening, the Viceroy was to make an important announcement. That's what Lala Kanshi Ram told his wife Prabha Rani, whose education had become his task. Lala Kanshi Ram was not too literate himself—it is doubtful if he ever finished high school. But life had rolled him around, misfortunes had come and gone, and this had given an edge to his intelligence."[3]

The protagonist Lala Kanshi Ram is indirectly reflected through these lines. He is not highly educated but the socio-political trend of the time has sharpened the edge of his mind and broadened his sensibility. His life is limited to the small circle of his own business and his happy interactions with his family, friends and neighbours. His attitude towards the British Raj is marked with an element of ambiguity. On the one hand, he is moved by the patriotic feelings to free his country, on the other hand, he likes the pageants and processions, and safety and security of the British Raj. He fails to see the drastic dimensions of Hindu-Muslim hostility which is destined to take place in a few weeks. Thus, he is utterly shocked and dismayed by the events that follow and the dreadful reality of his having to leave his homeland comes to him as a bolt from the blue. The exodus of the people of the refugee camp, the painful experiences in the camp, the sad news of his dear daughter Madhu Bala's death are series of experiences that make his heart heavy and sadden his soul. But the protagonist in him is powerful as instead of getting down and defeated, he gains a heroic endurance.

> "Many parts of him had died, but there were others still alive, forcefully and affirmatively alive, and he knew he was not defeated."[4]

Lala learns to transcend the narrow ideal of communal harmony and his mind is now ruled by pity, compassion and love. The hardships that he faces to find accommodation in Delhi increases his moral responsibilities, and his sorrow over the death of Gandhi is deep and penetrating. His individual consciousness has in the end matured and developed into a national consciousness, rather we can say that he has attained a purely humanistic consciousness.

Lala Kanshi Ram is ambivalent in his attitude toward the conquerors of his country. For some of their qualities he has the highest admiration. But at the same time he is equally critical of their many faults and failings. He admired the British for bringing some kind of peace to India, for their pageantry, precision, impartiality, efficiency in administration and controlling situations and taking action during crisis:

> "But deeper down, he also admired the British, in any case he enjoyed the safety of the British Raj and hugged it lovingly. All said and done, the British had brought some kind of peace to his torn land. Think of the Sikhs after Maharaja Ranjit Singh—or the Marathas. Think of the Muslims in Delhi or in the Deccan [...]"[5]

Lala Kanshi Ram believed that the English could control any situation effectively. When Lala heard about the communal riots, he thought how his friend the English Superintendent of

Police who had been transferred would have dealt effectively with this difficult situation:

> "Leave it to the English to handle emergencies, he murmured to himself. And he also saw the English Superintendent receiving a medal for bravery at a colourful parade afterwards."[6]

But later, this spell of the British in the mind of Lala is dispelled when the partition of India could not be avoided in any way and at any cost. Lala Kanshi Ram with others like Lala Radhey Shyam, Lala Banarsi Das and Lala Shamsher Bahadur, knew that Mahatma Gandhi would save them. They thought that the Viceroy broadcast would say nothing new. The British who had all along spoken of unity and of a united India could not do anything now and change the minds of the people. There was nothing to despair about hard reality. The Muslim merchants knew that Pakistan was a certainty. When all the tenants assembled in Bibe Amar Vati's room to listen to the radio broadcast, they were discussing the burning problem of the day. Soon it was Pandit Nehru's voice coming through the radio. He had been acting as Prime Minister of the Interim Government since September 1946 and his voice had boomed on the air many a time in the last nine months but never before had he sounded so tired:

> "He was a brilliant leader, a very proud leader and in leading the motley millions of his people, people speaking many tongues, living in such diverse climes, having such diverse customs and habits, in leading these millions to a single, united goal, he had a right to be impatient with them, to be abrupt [...]."[7]

The feelings of the people roused as soon as his broadcast was over. They were not interested in what Jinnah or Baldeo Singh were to say. The radio was switched off. Lala Kanshi Ram was there with the people. They looked at each other, and more than regret and fear on the face of each one of them, was distrust and disbelief. When the radio was on again, all of them heard Jinnah finishing his speech with his last words 'Pakistan Zindabad! Long live Pakistan.' Eears prevailed once again and they could not believe that the Congress had agreed to this partition.

The same night the Muslims in the city were celebrating the partition. There were illuminations and processions. Sialkot was a Muslim majority city and many Hindu mohallas had installed gates to protect themselves. Arun, Niranjan and Suraj Prakash were apprehensive of a visit from some prehistoric monster,

> "The procession came down Trunk Bazaar, and stopped outside the eastern entrance to the street. It was a wild sight. The mob was in a transport which exceeded pain or hysteria. As far as you could see, the bazaar was a sea of heads. They were split into many small groups, and before each group there were two or three drummers [...]. Many of them were dancing the Bhangra, the Punjab dance of Victory [...]. And together they shouted, 'Pakistan Zindabad! Long live Pakistan.'"[8]

The very next day, the Viceroy announced in a press conference that the date of freedom would be declared a little later because of the appointment of a boundary commission to decide the precise boundaries of Pakistan and India. Lala Kanshi Ram was very hopeful that Sialkot, his hometown, would never go to Pakistan side. But this wish proved futile and remained unfulfilled.

Arun, Kanshi Ram's son, was feeling very hopeless. Arun and Nur, the daughter of Choudhari Barkat Ali, were in the same college and both of them were like minded youths. They were deeply in love with each other. For the sake of Nur, Arun was prepared to embrace Islam, he could embrace even death. But the politicians were coming in his way. He knew the conspiracy of the politicians behind the whole move:

> "Jinnah and Liaquat Ali Khan were coming into an estate; as was Nehru. Why else would they rush into Azadi at this pace—an Azadi which would ruin the land and destroy its unity? For the creation of Pakistan solved nothing. One would have to go around with tweezers through all the villages to separate the Muslims from the Hindus. Arun knew this, the game of which he and Nur and millions like them were only victims. But politicians gave ideas legs, even through they were the wrong kind of ideas [...]."[9]

Later, the situation worsened. Lala Kanshi Ram was not willing to leave his home to go to the refugee camp. There was no point in leaving. Arun had been to the store with his father, but he returned home at noon. Lala Kanshi Ram returned in the night with a heavy heart saying that his store had been looted. He was standing stunned and strange ideas were coming to his mind. In the meantime Choudhari Barkat Ali informed him that their street was to be looted that night and the Deputy Commissioner was murdered last night by a Muslim body-guard. Lala Kanshi Ram wanted to tell that the Congress Muslims in the city had become powerless to prevent mass violence. Lala thus decided to go to the refugee camp as it was safer than undertaking a journey to Amritsar.

After a few days in the camp Lala Kanshi Ram was informed by Dr. Chander Bhan of his daughter Madhu Bala's killing by an irritate mob in a train while coming to Sialkot. Madhu's death crushed the whole family. One after the other, many adverse things befell him during these three months, circumstances in which Kanshi Ram was a loser, yet he was not defeated. He was benumbed by the event, he fretted, but the next moment Arun could see him pulling his shoulders up. Like the cornered Oedipus, he followed lead after lead. He trusted the police, the army and the leaders when they offered to protect him. But one after the other, all of Lala's trusts had come to nothing:

> "Each passing day narrowed further his chances of living in the land he loved so much. What the leaders of India were offering the people of the Punjab was an enormous bluff, he felt. They had neither the power nor the intention of maintaining the minorities in their homes, they had not the power of saving their lives [...]. Jinnah and Nehru were villains enough [...]."[10]

After the Boundary Commission's award was announced on 17 August, every one knew where he stood—on a part of Pakistan, or of India. Violence in the Punjab reached an unprecedented pitch after the announcement of the award. For Lala there was no way out but to leave the land with the members of his family. He managed to move into the already packed tents. From Dera

Baba Nanak, Lala's family moved swiftly to Amritsar and from there as swiftly to Delhi.

Lala Kanshi Ram had agreed to come to Delhi as it was the seat of the Government. All the leaders lived there and he found the thought, exciting. He also thought that there would be opportunities for starting a good business. But his welcome was bleak. He saw only unknown and unfriendly faces on the platform. It took him several hours to reach the officials receiving the incoming refugees. Lala could not get accommodation for his family and the people with him. For the next three days he searched every single locality in Delhi. He dared not go to New Delhi, but he visited each of the areas in old Delhi. The family stayed at the Railway Station. Thus, moving from place to place in search of accommodation, Lala got tired and pale and now it seemed there was no blood left in him. Never before in his life had he felt so exposed, so naked and so defenceless:

> "He wanted no more of that. He wanted a name for himself once again—not fame, just a name. And the wind that blew nonstop through those tents, it had driven holes through his body. He wanted walls around himself and doors and he wanted a bed to lie on and clean sheets and he wanted Prabha Rani to be alone with him [...]."[11]

Once again in the Custodian's office, Lala Kanshi Ram tried his best. There he tried in vain to conceal his tears which were brimming over his eyes. He was weeping openly. His watery eyes looked through space at nothing. Arun felt that his father could find a house. That evening they moved to Kingsway Camp on Alipur Road. They were now in brick hutments and not in tents. He did not give up his attempts to find out a permanent house allotted by the Rehabilitation Office and for this he visited 'P' Block several times which was the seat of the Delhi Administration. While coming back home at Kingsway Camp busstop, he sensed much tension in the bazaar. Reaching the camp, he was told of Gandhiji's assassination by a fanatic Hindu. He heard Jawahar Lal Nehru on air:

> "It was no ordinary light, he said, it was a most extraordinary flame. It was gone and India was plunged into darkness [...]."[12]

Thus, the politicians made Lala Kanshi Ram a nowhere man, a castaway alongwith a number of people like him as houseless wretches and refugees. In the name of "Azadi" they played different roles and partitioned India into two nations—India and Pakistan. Thus, one can sum up in a single simple sentence that *Azadi is not only the story of Lal Kanshi Ram but millions of people like him.*

REFERENCES

1. Nahel was born in 1927 at Sialkot (now in Pakistan).
2. Chaman Nahal, *Three Contemporary Novelists* (New Delhi: Classical Publishing Co. 1985), 39.
3. —— Azadi (Delhi: Vision Books, 1979), 1.
4. *Azadi*, 269.
5. *Azadi*, 269.
6. *Azadi*, 31.
7. *Azadi*, 64.
8. *Azadi*, 72.
9. *Azadi*, 96.
10. *Azadi*, 210.
11. *Azadi*, 350.
12. Nahel, *The Crown and the Loincloth* (New Delhi: Vikas Publishing House, 1981), 111.

2

Raja Rao and The Frontiers of Fiction

RATRI RAY

The aim of this essay is not to analyse what Raja Rao wrote, but what he did not write, in *The Serpent and the Rope*. An attempt will be made at defining one of the frontiers of fiction and see how, in not going beyond this limit, Raja Rao has shown himself a true artist. Put more concisely, this essay seeks to prove that *The Serpent and the Rope* is not a mystical novel. Indeed, I am convinced that the phrase 'mystical novel' is a contradiction in terms, an oxymoron, an impossibility.

We have come a long way from *Dapnis and Chloe*, and seen the novel take many different forms. In this respect the novel is a truly protean genre. We have read straightforward narration with delight and many a gentle reader has gone through a mixture of first-person and third-person narration as in *Bleak House*. The novel form has been taken to the limits of coherence by *Finnegans Wake* and of late the long-suffering reader has been subjected to novels like *The Golden Gate* and *A Suitable Boy*. We have read novels in the form of marginalia in Nabokov's virtuoso performance *Pale Fire* and it can now be said that no limits can be imposed on the form and technique of the novel, provided the narrative interest is there. The technique, naturally, includes the style—for example, the stream-of-consciousness method is a technique as well as a style. If what James called the Commanding Centre—the compositional centre of the novel, is a firm and unified one—then the ingenuity of the writer may have full play and the novel still remain a novel.

This, however, cannot be said of the raw material of novels. Fiction, more than any other literary form, is "an imitation of life, an image of truth, a mirror of custom." This much quoted tricolon had been applied to comedy by Cicero, but it is equally applicable to novels. A novelist attempts to hold up a mirror, and present a faithful picture of men and manners. Whatever technique the novel employs, ranging from the omniscient author technique to the stream-of-consciousness, the fact remains that it is a picture of life, a 'fictive picture' according to James. This is so much in the nature of a platitude that there is no need to labour the point or cite examples or quote authorities. Whatever the time or the place, the characters in a novel are persons we recognise and sometimes identify ourselves with. The experiences they undergo, the agonies and ecstacies that play kaleidoscopically in their lives are such as come within the perspective of human understanding. "Nothing human is alien to me"—says the novelist and the reader echoes him, whether the novelist is Petrous or Cervantes or Lawrence.

It is here that one of the frontiers of fiction can be marked. Just as nothing human is alien to the novelist, so, that which is beyond human experience is beyond his pale. At this point an objection might be raised: how to regard works like *Black Beauty* or *Flush* ? Now, the former should not be dismissed as children's literature, for whether it is meant for adults or for children, the problem remains the same. It can be safely affirmed that these works fall definitely within the periphery of the novel. Although the experiences are those of a non-human creature, yet, for the moment, the reader must willingly suspend his disbelief and establishe identification with the narrator or the protagonist as the case may be. In the case of a satirical allegory like *Animal Farm*, again, one experiences no difficulty in calling it a novel, since the real life parallel is all too evident. *Moby Dick* likewise presents no problems, for the reader recognises a symbol when he sees it, and the human characters in it are sympathetic ones, though the experience of whaling might be an unfamiliar one. Such is the flexibility of the novel that it can encompass all such offshoots provided (1) the narrative interests the reader and (2) human experiences are there. These are the two elements that can be taken as the lowest common denominators of all novels, irrespective of the technique employed, the locale described and the characters adopted by the writer. Without these basic factors a novel cannot be designated as such.

What, then, about the experience of mystics? *The Serpent and the Rope* is reputedly a spiritual autobiography. K.R.S. Iyengar takes up the three novels—*Kanthapura, The Serpent and the Rope* and *The Cat and Shakespeare*—and considers them as a trilogy, comparing them with *The Divine Comedy*. Logically enough in this scheme *The Serpent and the Rope* takes the position of *Purgatorio*: "There are glimpses of Inferno's circles and Purgatory's slopes in *Kanthapura* and *The Serpent and the Rope* respectively."[1] Other critics play variations on the same theme:

> In *The Serpent and the Rope* he deals with the metaphysical quest for absolute truth when man can distinguish the rope for the serpent.[2]

S.C. Harrex's students, overawed by the novel, had reacted to it in many different ways, but all of them had laid stress on the spiritual aspect. It is true that Harrex does not deliver a personal opinion, but his extensive quotations from and comments on the papers submitted by his students serve to convey the impression that it was the philosophical or the spiritual content of the novel that had elicited the most emphatic response from these young readers.[3]

Let us conclude with a more sophisticated opinion—that of H.M. Williams:

> It is essentially therefore a spiritual odyssey [...]. Like Raja Rao's *The Serpent and the Rope* [...] the novel of spiritual quest in India.[4]

These few opinions taken at random out of scores of others, amply illustrate, if illustration be needed, the indisputably spiritual quality of the novel. As far as internal evidence is concerned, almost any page of the text, opened at random, will illustrate the point. A little further on in the present essay these will be provided when the text is being discussed. Apart from the philosophical dialogues, musings and the significant events occurring in the novel, there is biographical support for looking upon *The Serpent* as a mystical or at least spiritual novel. Raja Rao himself has said:

> *The Serpent and the Rope* came as a result of spiritual fulfilment—that is to say it was born after I had met my guru.[5]

As such one finds *The Serpent* a novel which has intensely philosophical, even spiritual leanings, but is still firmly anchored to the bedrock of reality. The question is—how intense is this philosophical quality? Can it be said to be mystical or even spiritual? If so, how far has it progressed along the via mystica?

For determining this a cursory glance at mysticism is necessary. The subject has a vast and profound literature which ranges, in Europe, alone, from first-hand experience of mystics like St. Dionysius in the fifth century and Thomas Merton in the present, to the work of theorists like St. Thomas Aquinas of the thirteenth century and William James in the present one. This has its oriental counterpart and in India we have mystical literature from the Upanishads down to Sri Aurobindo. A few examples will have to suffice. Different writers have given different characteristics of mysticism. William James for example, gives ineffability, poetic quality, passivity and transiency as four marks of the mystical state.[6] These need not concern us: for our present purposes it can be firmly stated that whatever else it might be, mystical experience is definitely an other-worldly one. The mystic, dedicated to a life whose ultimate aim is union with the Absolute (Christ, God, Brahman or any other supreme entity) almost always leads an ascetic life withdrawn from ordinary society. Thus, the unknown author of *The Cloud of Unknowing* advises the aspirant:

> Try to forget all created things He ever made and the purpose behind them so that your thought and longing does not turn or reach out to them either in general or in particular.[7]

Del Maestro in his introduction to *The Revelations of Dame Juliana* gives a list of all the notable events of her time :

> The Black Death (from 1348), part of the Hundred Years' War (1337-1453), the Peasants' Revolt (1381), [...] all took place within the lifetime of Juliana. Yet no hint of these momentous events appear in her book.[8]

St. John of Cross describes the withdrawn state of the mystic in one of his poems:

> I entered in—I know not where —
> And there remaining, knew no more
> Transcending far all human lore.[9]

Instances can be multiplied and these few serve to illustrate the point adequately. The mystic is not concerned with that which surrounds him and oblivious of everything leads a life of contemplation. Of course there are a few exceptions. Not all mystics lived in deserts or cloisters—Jacob Boehme was a shoemaker. Many mystics came back to ordinary life after achieving their goal and tried to lead men along the right path. Evenly Underhill calls these active mystics like St. Teresa (1515-1582) and Swami Vivekananda 'the Ambassadors to the Absolute. But in the beginning of their life they too had to withdraw into solitude and meditation. The fact that the mystical way of life diverges widely from ordinary life is almost of a self-evident truth. It logically follows therefore that a novel cannot be a mystical one. This is a clearly defined frontier of fictional narrative.

Another quality, as universally accepted as that of otherwordliness, is ineffability. The mystical experience is entirely spiritual and has no satisfactory parallel in real life. The mystic therefore, though desperately trying to communicate, can at best hope to impart but a frail distorted shadow of his intense experience. Yes, the experiences are intense ones. In one of his numerous sonnets Sri Aurobindo says:

> The world's happiness flows through me like wine
> Its million sorrows are my agonies.[10]

Such lines (once read never forgotten), seem to belie the assertion that mystical experience is ineffable. Yet not every mystic is a poet and these lines can but convey an infinitesimal part of Sri Aurobindo's experience. Most of the time the mystics try to solve the problem of communication by using symbols, yet as St. John of Cross points out:

> The soul can never attain to the height of the divine union so far as it is possible in this life, through the meditation of any forms or figures.[11]

Again therefore, it seems inevitable that a novel cannot express mystical experiences, even through symbols.

It remains to point out the different stages of mystical life. These are usually supposed to be three in number. Every mystic has to follow his own tortuous path towards his goal, rising and falling and rising again on the rocky and thorny tract. Yet after studying their progress certain definite stages can be distinguished. St. Dionysius says in his *Mystical Theology*:

> Three-fold is the way to God. The first is the way of purification, the second the way of illumination, the third the way of union.[12]

Besides these, two more have been added by scholars, The Awakening of the Soul coming before these three and The Dark Night of the Soul occurring later. The Oriental mysticism, that of tótal annihilation of the self has been added. This states 'the Eighth Stage of Progress' according to the Sufis. Nirvana according to the Buddhists, has been described by Shankaracharya and the relevant lines quoted in *The Serpent* (114).

As this essay is not a treatise on mysticism, these stages are not described. The only reason they have been mentioned at all is because the novel does not describe the hero as passing through these. As a matter of fact, it brings the hero only to the first stage, The Awakening of the Soul.

Now that the preliminaries are over, it behoves us to reaffirm certain ideas, namely: the qualities of otherworldliness and ineffability make mysticism one of the subjects that cannot be treated in a novel which is by its nature a description of men and manners, a description of human experiences.

Looking now at *The Serpent* we find that the hero is a highly intellectual young man who is, to use a cliche, in search of his soul. He has been brought up in the intellectual diet of the Upanishads and other Sanskrit literatures. The Upanishads are among the oldest mystical literature of the world, but familiarity with them does not mean that he understands them. Who, indeed, can truly understand them unless he is a mystic himself? Ramaswamy is familiar with other Sanskrit works as well—they have formed and moulded his personality. He has an aesthetic and intellectual apprehension of them and such works are an integral part of his life. Here are a few quotations:

> I even knew Grammar and the Brahman Sutras, read the Upanishads at the age of four.
>
> We had one thing in common: we both knew Sanskrit, and could entertain each other with Uttarramcharita or Raghuvansha.
>
> For hour after hour I chanted verses, especially those of Bharatihari, Kalidasa or Shankara.[13]

Ramaswamy settles in France, marries a French girl and begins to work on a thesis on the religious principles of the Cathers, comparing them with Vedanta. So in addition to his knowledge of Indian philosophy, he comes into contact with Western religious thought as well. He is an intellectual par excellance. No wonder the novel has been branded as 'difficult'—containing as it does, passages and dialogues on obscure Christian doctrines as well as on Vedanta. It is loaded—even overloaded, with philosophy.

Not only Rama, but the other characters as well, are either learned or philosophical introverts. Georges and Lezo, two of Rama's friends, are forever arguing, or expounding, obscure religious or philosophical ideas. Madeleine, Rama's wife, is at first a highly intellectual introvert, but inspite of this, a loving wife:

> I love you Rama, with a strange, distant, impenitent love —as though in loving you I say 'I don't in fact love you.[14]

It seems Rama can lead a happy domestic life, (though rather highbrow) with her:

> I kissed her with warmth, certitude and devotion. She was the tabernacle of my habitation, I would build a paraclete yet.[15]

This however is not enough. Raja Rao wants her to proceed towards a spiritual life on her own—completely independent of Rama. He is cruel enough to make her undergo the gruelling experience of a miscarriage, after which she gradually turns her back to life, and, embracing Buddhism, leads the life of an ascetic.

It is not that there are no ordinary worldly characters in the novel. Raja Rao has given quite a few such characters, particularly Madeleine's uncle and aunt and Uncle Seetharamu, their Indian counterpart, but such characters exist only as props to the main characters.

Rama comes twice to India, once on the occasion of his father's death and again at the time of his sister's marriage. He has extra-marital love affairs with two girls, Savithri and Lakshmi, and at the end of the novel his marriage is dissolved. There is thus, a story in the novel, interspersed with philosophical passages and dialogues. Raja Rao does not shine as a balled-maker, but the novel does not lack narrative interest which is one of the basic requirements of such works.

The characters, as mentioned above, are not such as are commonly met with, but they are human enough. Though Rama is such an awe-inspiring intellectual, he has human qualities and undergoes experiences that are recognisably human ones. It might be difficult for the common reader to establish identification with him, yet the reader can easily take Rama for an intellectual and relegate his thoughts and emotions to such individuals. The novel, though it might not give a faithful picture of the social life of India or of France, still presents human experiences.

The philosophical discussions (the best known is the passage in which the meaning behind the title is explained are on 335), as well as Rama's own thoughts take up a major portion of the novel. As we go through the book a clear picture of Rama's tortured soul emerges. He is a man torn by conflicting ideas. On the one hand, he is a loving son and brother, an ordinary married man not above enjoying a clandestine love affair. On the other hand, he is in quest of peace and spiritual fulfilment. Quite early in the book he says:

> Life is a pilgrimage, I know, but a pilgrimage to where—and of what?[16]

Now the symbol of pilgrimage is quite a common one in mysticism. Irrespective of time, space and religious doctrine, the mystic's life has been compared with a pilgrimage. This should not make us think that Rama is thinking like a dedicated mystic here, for, apart from all esoteric associations, life is compared to a pilgrimage by non-mystical persons as well. In this instance Rama is talking and thinking like a layman, an intellectual puzzled by the complexities of life. There is no such puzzlement in a true mystic who sees his goal shining clearly before him and flies single-mindedly towards it. Rama does not as yet know what he wants. This indeterminate state persists throughout the book. One comes across highly philosophy discussions and there are quite a few instance which can be construed as having mystical, or at least spiritual, connotations. Thus, after a long discussion with Georges, Rama is in an uplifted mood and chants the verses of Shankaracharya that record the ineffable experience of union with Brahman (114). Rama, however exalted he might be, is still an ordinary man with longings for spiritual development. He has not taken the all-important step that would transform or turn him into the kind of man who occupies the highest position in the world—a mystic.

It is much later in the book that a decisive moment comes. Gradually his burning questions, his self-searchings, his searing uncertainty bear fruit. The first stage of mystical life is reached—The Awakening of the soul. This stage is not included within the via mystica by St. Dionysius. Actually speaking it is the beginning of the mystical life. The individual who has been leading an ordinary life realises the worthlessness of that life, the existence of a higher Reality and determines to devote himself to the attainment of union with that Reality. In some mystics this is a sudden, shattering experience, as in St. Paul and Pascal. In others it is a gradual awakening as in Geroge Fox. In Rama's case it seems to have been the latter, reaching a culmination at the end of the book. Even in the entry from his diary, dated 27-3-54, he is still without direction though he has taken the right decision:

> Yes, I say to myself, "I must leave this world, I must leave, leave this world." But, Lord, where shall I go, where?[17]

Finally, in the last entry, the awakened soul sets out firmly towards the destined goal:

> No, not a God, but a Guru is what I need. "O Lord, my Guru, my Lord," I cried, in the middle of this dreadful winter night.[18]

He decides to go to Travancore and the book, most appropriately, ends where the real journey of a mystic begins.

No mean artist, Raja Rao has written a novel that keeps within the limits of the genre, and, when the time comes when it must cross the frontiers of fiction into the uncharted continents of mystical life, he wisely brings it to a close. The novel remains a novel—a record of human experiences, dealing with two different countries and cultures, presenting a gallery of characters, narrating a story from the commanding centre of Rama's consciousness. It is a 'bildungs-roman' presenting the growth of an individual. It ends at that precise point where Rama's life as an individual ends and his life as a mystic begins. Raja Rao does not try to present the spiritual, other-worldly experiences of the life he is to begin. *The Serpent and the Rope* is a novel, but not a mystical novel.

REFERENCES

1. Iyengar, K.R.S., *Indian Writing in English*? (Sterling Pubs., 4th. edn. 1984), 411.
2. Raizada, H., *Literature as Sadhana* in Sharma, K.K. ed. *Indo-English Literature* (Vimal Prakashan, Ghaziabad, 1977), 165-173.
3. *Ibid.*, 178-192.
4. Williams, H.M., *Indo-Anglian Literature 1800-1970* (Orient Longman, 1976), 63-96.
5. Quoted by Raizada, *op. cit.* 159.

6. James, W., *Varieties of Religious Experience* (New American Library, New York, 1958.
7. Wolters, C., transl. *The Cloud of Unknowing* (Penguin, 1974), 53.
8. Del Maestro, M.L., ed. *The Revelations of Dame Juliana of Norwich*, (Image Books, New York, 1977), 11.
9. Peers, E. Allison, Transl. *St. John of the Cross, Complete Works* (Burns Oates and Wasbourne Ltd., London, 1947), Vol. II, 448.
10. Sri Aurobindo, *Collected Poems* (Sri Aurobindo Ashram) Pondicherry, 1972), 142.
11. Peers *op. cit.*, *The Ascent Mount Carmel*, 133.
12. Woods, R. ed. *Understanding Mysticism* (Image Books New York, 1980) 33.
13. Rao, R., *The Serpent and the Rope*, (Orient Pbks., Delhi, no date) 5, 31, 70. All quotations are from this edition.
14. *Ibid.*, 40.
15. *Ibid.*, 230
16. *Ibid.*, 26.
17. *Ibid.*, 399.
18. *Ibid.*, 403.

3

Theme and Form in R.K. Narayan's *The Man Eater of Malgudi*

SANGITA NAGPAL

Critical opinion usually dubs R.K. Narayan as a small town ironist laughing at small town eccentrics, a delightful local colourist and an amused observer of life and manners. An intensive analysis of a novel like *The Man Eater of Malgudi*, reveals quite a different Narayan—a writer who not only asks some fundamental questions about good and evil and their roles in human life, but also finds answers to them. In doing so, he grafts a realistic narrative of modern South Indian life on an ancient Hindu myth, thus ensuing that his questionings and solutions are firmly rooted in his own cultural ethos, a consummation which should be the sole raison d'etre of any Indian fiction in English that hopes to endure as something more than an interesting literary freak.

The Man Eater of Malgudi is at once a re-creation of the old Hindu myth of Bhasmasura in modern form, a myth presented with both serious parallelism and ironic contrast in the manner of William Faulkner and a presentation of two diametrically opposed attitudes to life. The Bhasmasura Parallel is clearly indicated in the novel in more than one place, by Sastri, who tells Natraja the narrator, less than half way through the story that Vasu "shows all the definitions of a rakshasa—a demoniac creature who possessed enormous strength, strange powers and genius, but recognized no sort of restraints of man or God"[1] (95-96).

He adds: "Every rakshasha gets swollen with his ego. He thinks he is invincible, beyond every law. But sooner or later something or other will destroy him"[2] (96). This principle he illustrates from the story of Bhasmasura "who acquired a special boon that everything he touched should be scorched, while nothing could destroy him. He made humanity suffer. God Vishnu was incarnated as a dancer of great beauty, named Mohini, with whom the asura became infatuated. She promised to yield to him only if he imitated all the gestures and movements of her own dancing. At one point in the dance Mohini placed her palms on her head, and the demon followed this gesture in complete forgetfulness and was reduced to ashes that very second, the blighting touch becoming active on his own head"[3] (96-7).

The second reference to the Bhasmasura myth comes right at the end of the novel, when in the last paragraph Sastri points out to Natraja the moral of Vasu's sudden and violent end:

"Every demon appears in the world with a special boon of indestructibility. Yet the universe has survived all the rakshasas that were ever born. Every demon carries within him unknown to himself, a tiny seed of self destruction, and goes up in thin air at the most unexpected moment. Otherwise what is to happen to humanity?"[4] (242).

Vasu is indeed the perfect embodiment of the typical rakshasa of ancient Hindu mythology. The raksha so is always pictured as a being of super human strength, ugly and ferocious in appearance, with cannibalistic propensities, incapable of affection, gratitude, sympathy, or regard for others and in fact revelling in inflicting pain; a nocturnal creature, a creature of the jungle, full of mystery; dirty and unclean in habits, and a being completely amoral; obeying no laws of God or man.

The description of the rakshasa fits Vasu perfectly in all respects. His very appearance is rakshasa like 'A large man about six feet tall,' he has a 'bull neck,' a 'tanned face,' a 'hammer fist,' large powerful eyes under thick eyebrows, a large forehead, and a shock of unkempt hair, 'like a black hat.' His clothes, loud and gaudy, (red check bush-shirt and field-grey trousers) are all of a piece with his appearance, so is his vehicle a jeep which he drives at breakneck speed. Natraja aptly describes him as 'the prince of darkness' (214).[5] His movements are as mysterious as his activities in the jungle. He is a taxi dermist (a profession that clearly puts him in the category of those outside the pale of civilization, according to ancient Hindu belief), and his room is filled with a strong smell of rotting flesh and hides being cured—which does not disturb him in the least. Vasu, appropriately nick-named "Man eater" by Natraj, has the strength of a rakshasa also, illustrated clearly by the story of his training under the Pahelwan (wrestler) (16).[6] His diet than consisted of one hundred almonds every morning with half a seer of milk and six eggs with honey, followed by chicken and rice for lunch and vegetables and fruits at night. Rigorous exercises starting at three o'clock in the morning coupled with this diet gave him a giant's strength within six months. His feats of strength included splintering a three inch panel of seasoned teak with his fist, snapping chairs, twisting iron bars and pulverizing granite[7] (16). Later in the story he breaks his bedstead with a single blow of his fist, dislocates the wrist of the policeman with a single strike and kills himself when he hits himself on the temple to crush a mosquito.

Vasu does not only have a rakshasa's strength, he uses it like a rakshasa also. Boorish and unmannerly rude and aggressive, he bullies and brow beats people. 'I challenge any man to contradict me'[8] (15) is his motto. Callous and hard-hearted, he is absolutely incapable of any regard for others and their feelings and needs in fact, he seems to take a perverse pleasure in making people suffer. Fro instance, he takes Natraja with him to the Mempi forest and abandons him there, even ignoring him when the poor man, hungry and tired, asks him for money; he shoots the pet dog of a small boy and horrifies the entire town by shooting an eagle and announcing his plan to shoot the temple elephant. He seems to be perfectly immune to all human emotions and feelings. Love for him is mere lust—hence, the many and various women who ascend his staircase at night. Children only bore him; when Natraja tries to introduce him to his little boy Vasu briskly says. 'Now, go away, boy'[9] (19). Ingratitude a special characteristic of the rakshasa mentality (as revealed in the legend of Bhasmasura, who threatened to destroy the very benefactor who had given him the wonderful boon) is another of Vasu's traits. The only homage he pays to the Guru who trained him is contained in his own words. "I knew his weak spot. I hit him there with the edge of my palm with a chopping movement and he fell down and squirmed on the floor." The recollection of this incident moves him to laughter. Later, he repays Natraja's hospitality by harassing him in several ways.

Vasu revels in breaking all laws and is a law unto himself. He tells Natraja that as a young man he participated in the Civil Disobedience Movement (perhaps it was disobedience of law and not so much love of the motherland that prompted him to do it). As a hunter he has a licence to shoot only ducks and deer, but he shoots all animals, including a tiger. He offers to collect donations for the poet, bullies people into paying ['One will have to sell the vessels in the kitchen and find the money, only to be rid of him'[10] (150) is the popular reaction], and then embezzles the entire amount.

Lastly, far from being an unlettered barbarian, Vasu is actually an M.A. in History, Economics and Literature, and to make this combination still more strange, has also studied taxidermy under an expert. He is proud of his skill and tells Natraja, "After all we are civilized human beings, educated and cultured, and it is up to us to prove our superiority to nature. Science conquers nature in a new way every day; why not in creation also? That's my philosophy"[11] (15). Later he declares: 'I admire people with a scientific outlook'[12] (175). He justifies his plan to shoot the temple elephant thus, "There's nothing terrible in shooting. You pull your trigger and out goes the bullet, and at the other end there is an object waiting to receive it. It is just give and take"[13] (176). He has even written a book on wild life, with two chapters devoted to animal behaviour.

Vasu is thus a complete rakshasa and the close parallel between his story and the Bhasmasura myth is very clear, as pointed out by Sastri. Bhasmasura was given his boon by Shiva, the most powerful of Gods; Vasu is befriended by Natraja (which is also one of the numerous names of Shiva) but Natraja is a perfect contrast to Shiva, the God of destruction, for he is only a weak, timid, harmless creature. One version of the Bhasmasura legend has it that the demon was suddenly born out of the sweat of Shiva as the God was dancing. Vasu's appearance in Malgudi is equally sudden, but Natraja is in no way responsible for it. Once he gets his boon Bhasmasura starts persecuting men and Gods, even committing sacrilege, Vasu makes a general nuisance of himself in Malgudi but is killed before he can actually commit the sacrilege he has planned. Bhasmasura was destroyed by Vishnu, who took the form of the beautiful damsel Mohini, and artfully tricked him into the suicidal action. Vasu is destroyed not so much by Rangi as through her, for she is only an unconscious instrument of his destruction. She is to fan him while he keeps his vigil, but drops off to sleep thus allowing the mosquitoes to pester Vasu who deals himself his own death blow. The name 'Rangi' is obviously derived from Ranganath, one of the appellations of Vishnu, but the contrast between Mohini and Rangi is replete with irony. Mohini is a divine damsel, Rangi, a poor temple dancer whose morals are universally suspect. Mohini was a perfection of feminine beauty; Rangi is only a perfect female animal[14] (109). There is a persistent inter weaving of serious parallelism and ironic contrast in *The Man Eater of Malgudi.*

The interplay between Vasu and Natraja also indicates a contrast between two diametrically opposed attitudes to life, each shown to be disastrous in its own way, between the demoniacal, self centered egotism of Vasu and the ineffectual, self-effacing altruism of Natraja, between the temerity of Vasu and the timidity of Natraja. For Vasu, everything in the external world must subserve his own interests. Other people, society, human considerations—all exist to feed his egotism. Such an attitude to life is fraught with obvious dangers for both the individual and society; such self centredness must inevitably end in self destruction, for true to its nature, it must generate from within itself the forces which destroy it. Natraja's altruism is as extreme as Vasu's egotism. It makes him unwordly and unbusiness like in his own profession. His rival, the owner of the star printing press, has an original Heidelberg machine and Natraja is more proud of it than the owner himself. His salesmanship too is extremely queer. If business rests upon the principle that one makes people buy things they don't need by high pressure salesmanship, Natraja's way of doing business is most unorthodox. When Vasu wants five hundred visiting cards printed, Natraja suggests that he get only one hundred so that they keep fresh! When K.J. places a big order for labels for aerated water bottles, Natraja must neglect it, since he is busy with printing the poet's book, free of cost. Natraja is indeed so altruistic that he must always volunteer to do things for others, with considerable inconveniance to himself and make promises in good faith that he is sometimes unable to fulfil. He is a thoroughly ineffectual angel of mercy. When Vasu shoots a boy's pet dog, Natraja promises to give 'a beautiful black dog' to the boy, saying that it is 'the easiest thing'. He adds: 'I know many planters who have dogs, and I can always get a puppy for our little friend' (91-2).[15] Several days and numerous reminders later, the little friend realizes that the 'beautiful black dog' is never going to materialize. On the day of the procession, Natraja with his burning altruistic zeal, has, like Shakespeare's Bottom, offered to play several parts and do all kinds of jobs, so that in the end he realizes that he can get through it all only if he devotes four minutes to each task'. He cannot achieve this superhuman feat, and the only contribution he is able to make to the procession is that he faints away and creates a panic among his friends.

This excessive altruism is perhaps the result of an extreme congenital timidity and weakness in Natraja. As he ruefully admits. "The trouble with me was that I was not able to say 'no' to anyone and that got me into complications with everyone"[16] (207). Everyone bullies him, from the dare-devil Vasu down to his own assistant Sastri, who "did not care whether I had time for food or not-he was a tyrant when it came to printing labels, but there was no way of protesting"[17] (11). Like most timid people, Natraja has a lively, fertile imagination which can conjure up visions of possible disasters out of airy nothings. When Vasu forces him to accompany him to the Mempi forest, he is "struck with a sudden fear that this man was perhaps abducting me and was going to demand a ransom for releasing me from some tiger cave. What would my wife and little son do if they were suddenly asked to produce fifty thousand rupees for my release?"[18] (41). When a court summon arrives, he is convinced that he will land up in jail, and the picture of his destitute wife and child visiting him in prison "On permissible days" has already flashed upon his inward eye." Day dreaming is only the obverse of this passion for imaginary fears, an escape from a humdrum and ignoble reality. When he first meets Rangi face to face he lets his 'mind slide into a wild fantasy of seduction and passion.' He admits. 'I was no longer a married man with a child and home, I was an adolescent lost in dreams over a nude photograph'[19] (158). After he has ignominiously fainted in the crowd, he day dreams, in pure Walter Mitly fashion, of saving the day by a brilliant stroke of ingenuity. In the end, even the absurd idea that he had killed Vasu starts looking plausible to him. "If I have rid the world of Vasu, I have achieved something"[20] (237).

But this bravado cannot last long Reduced almost to the position of a social outcast, Natraja cannot bear his plight very long. He bursts into tears, as he laments. "This was the greatest act of destruction that the Man Eater had performed; he had destroyed my name, my friendships, and my world"[21] (239). Blind altruism has brought its own penalties. Normality is restored in the end when the secret of Vasu's death comes out, but it is obvious that Natraja has not learnt his lesson. His last remark, 'Yes, Sastri, I am at your service,' perhaps indicates that he is the same Natraja, Vasu or no Vasu, ready to be the cheerful victim of the next 'man eater' who might cross his path.

The golden mean between these contraries of self centred egotism and self effacing altruism is well represented by the level headed and mature Sastri. As a choric figure, he comments on both these attitudes and pinpoints their dangers. It is he who explains the Vasu phenomenon in terms of the rakshasa myth, as a devoted Hindu, he is convinced that like all rakshasas, Vasu too will meet his well deserved punishment some day. Throughout the narrative, the pious Sastri studiously keeps away from the ungodly Vasu and never speaks to him. This itself constitutes his judgement of Vasu. Vasu dead is as great a nuisance to Malgudi as Vasu living and Sastri scrupulously avoids both. As soon as the news of Vasu's death is out, Sastri goes on a pilgrimage, In the end, when Natraja has reached the nadir of despair, it is Sastri who consoles him and restores him to normalcy by revealing the secret of Vasu's death. With his solid common sense and staunch faith that evil, however triumphant, will ultimately destroy itself, Sastri appears to emphasize a way of life, straying away from which has brought death to Vasu and a great deal of mental anguish to Natraja.

Like most of Narayan's novels, *The Man Eater of Malgudi* is also a vision of life as a human comedy. The irony of the title is obvious enough. Here is a topsy turvy hunting yarn in which the strange 'man eater' kills himself, instead of being tracked and killed. We have also the usual crowd of eccentrics—Vasu and Natraja are, from one point of view, cases of comic abnormality, the poet (so much of a comic type that he actually has no name), writing the life of Lord Krishna in monosyllabic verse; Sen the journalist, an armchair politician whose bete noire is Nehru; the adjournment lawyer who is a specialist in prolonging a case beyond the wildest dreams of a litigant, the septuagenarian looking 'like a newborn infant when he bared his gums in a smile' the forest officer whose life's ambition is to compile a book of golden thoughts and the mahout who appears only once in the story and yet regales us with his entire autobiography[22] (127-28). In all these characters one sees Narayan's comic sense at its best. There is ample humour of situation too, arising mostly out of a sudden anticlimax, as in the scene when Natraja desperately creeps into Vasu's rooms determined to foil his shooting the elephant blissfully unaware that Vasu has been stone dead for some time. Narayan's verbal humour, resting upon quiet irony, lights up many a page, as in the tailor's view of Natraja as an abductor of elephants[23] (131), and in the description of Muthu pouring 'oblatory tea' into the disconsolate tailor's mouth, 'unwashed glass after unwashed glass'[24] (130).

But though the comedy is delightful, the Bhasmasura myth and the polarities representated by Vasu and Natraja emphasize sharply the moral issues involved here. The entire question of human relationships is dominated by a militant egotism which is evil and spreads suffering around and a timid altruism which submits tamely to evil. The remedy, as Sastri indicates, lies in respecting one's own individuality in taking a same, practical view of things, and in maintaining a firm faith in the divine dispensation which may allow evil to flourish for a time only to ensure that it destroys itself completely in the end. While the demon annihilates himself, and the ineffectual good angel potters blundering around, it is the same man with firm faith in God who enunciates the precepts and practice of the whole business of living.

REFERENCES

1. R.K. Narayan, *The Man Eater of Malgudi,* Indian Thought Publication, Mysore, 95-96. All quotations are from this edition.
2. *Ibid.*, 96.
3. *Ibid.*, 96-7.
4. *Ibid.*, 242.
5. *Ibid.*, 214.
6. *Ibid.*, 16.
7. *Ibid.*, 16.
8. *Ibid.*, 15.
9. *Ibid.*, 19.
10. *Ibid.*, 150.
11. *Ibid.*, 15.
12. *Ibid.*, 175.
13. *Ibid.*, 176.
14. *Ibid.*, 109.
15. *Ibid.*, 91-92.
16. *Ibid.*, 207.
17. *Ibid.*, p 11.
18. *Ibid.*, 41.
19. *Ibid.*, 158.
20. *Ibid.*, 237.
21. *Ibid.*, 239.
22. *Ibid.*, 127-28.
23. *Ibid.*, 131.
24. *Ibid.*, 130.

4

The Evolution of *The Guide*: The Individual —Society Equation in The Indian and The Western Contexts

ARUN SOULE

The Swami or Sanyasi motif is a fairly recurrent one in the novels of R.K. Narayan. Before the publication of *The Guide* in 1958, Narayan had used this effectively in *The Bachelor of Arts* (1937), where we saw the graduate Chandran, who after experiencing sensual pleasures in Madras, took refuge in the Kapleswar temple, where he eventually turned into a 'sanyasi.' A similar thing happens to Raju also in *The Guide,* who after an illicit relationship with Rosie and a brief stint in prison, finds himself in the role of a 'swami.' The difference, however, is that while Chandran returns back to the world to look after his household affairs, Raju reaches a point of no return.

In this paper an attempt will be made (1) to examine the role of the Community to see its influence on the individual (Raju) and (2) to compare the individual—society relationship between the Indian and the Western contexts.

In the Western context, especially in American Literature, many of the major writers have consistently expressed the view that society, more often than not, acts as a deterrent in an individual's personal development.

It is notable that even early writers like R.W. Emerson have been sharply critical of Society, and in the essay, "Self-Reliance" (1841), Emerson says:

> Society everywhere is in conspiracy against the manhood of every one of its members. Society is a joint-stock company [...]
>
> Who so would be a man must be a nonconformist. He who would gather immortal palms must not be hindered by the name of goodness, but must explore if it be goodness. Nothing is at last sacred but the integrity of your own mind. Absolve you to yourself, and you shall have the suffrage of the world (Emerson, 63-64).

A similar view has also been expressed by modern writers like Ernest Hemingway and Norman Mailer, though more emphatically. In his writings, Norman Mailer has expressed concern for the individual and the adverse effect that the repressive society has on him, which causes his spirit of creativity and romanticism to dry up and its place is taken up by a sense of conformity and fear. As Mailer admits to Richard Stern in an interview:

> The sickness of our times, for me, has been just this damn thing that everything has been getting smaller and smaller and less and less important, that the romantic spirit has dried up (Mailer, 305).

Mailer further emphasizes that if an individual does not defy the restrictive social norms, then he would be in danger of,

> a slow death by conformity with every creative instinct stifled (at what damage to the mind and the heart and the liver and the nerves no research foundation for cancer will discover in a hurry (Mailer, 271).

However, on examining the relationship between the individual (Raju) and the community in the Indian context, it is seen that in the initial stages, Raju falls in love with a married woman (Rosie), despite the advice of his friend, Gaffur or the warning of his mother to beware of "the snake woman." The inevitable happens and Marco abandons Rosie, who has no alternative but to go to Raju's house. Raju is alienated from his mother, his friends and his neighbours because society is not prepared to accept this adulterous relationship.

Raju's affair with Rosie is followed by other problems for Raju—the loss of his shop and physical humiliation; his quarrel with his creditor, the seth and his vindictive reaction; estrangement from friends like Gaffur, the driver; quarrel with his uncle; and the loss of his mother and the ancestral house.

Raju works hard to transform Rosie into the famous dancer—Nalini, but he has already taken the path of moral decline and falls prey to other vices like drinking and gambling. He has reached the stage where he is not above exploiting her talent for money and fame—which she resents, and they start mentally drifting apart. Raju's decline is complete when out of jealousy and emotional insecurity, he forges Marco's signature and ends up in prison.

Raju's degradation could obviously go no further, and his stint in prison is almost necessary for him to recover his sense of balance.

Raju's attempts at violating social norms result in alienation and suffering for him. Regarding the conservative norms of social life in India, Sudhir Kakkar elaborates;

> The Hindu view of action is necessarily a conservative one; it harks back to a 'golden age,' and harbours the sceptical conviction that social change is superfluous, an importunate deviation from traditional ways (Kakkar, 38).

On examining the second phase of Raju's life *i.e.,* when he comcs out of prison, and becomes a 'Swami' in the village, Mangala, it is seen that he does not repeat his earlier mistake of disregarding society while asserting his individuality. His movement through life is not alone, as he takes the village community of Mangala along with him. It is significant that on their part, the villagers and Velan (who represents the village community) accept Raju as a 'Swami' without asking any questions even though Raju is merely posing as a 'Swami'. Raju's encounter with Velan, initiates in him a process of self-recovery and becomes a movement in the opposite direction. If Rosie arouses Raju's sensuality and lust for power and money and alienates him from home and community, Velan, who symbolizes the unwavering faith of the villagers, directs Raju, albeit unconsciously, towards the path of self-discovery and self-transcendence. One of the deeper ironies of the novel is the reversal of the roles of the master and the disciple *i.e.*, between Raju and Velan, when Raju humbly confesses everything to Velan. It is to be noted that this is the same Raju who took the centrally placed sofa in the front row at Nalini's shows and wanted people to know that unless he sat there, Nalini would not be able to perform. This humility of Raju makes one realize the full impact of Velan's influence on him. Regarding the element of irony, which is present throughout the novel, and its connection with the events of the past, M.K. Naik says:

> This persistent juxtaposition of the present and the past not only underscores the irony of the central situation, but also shows with inexorable logic how the protagonist's present is rooted in the past and how the past also inevitably shapes his future (Naik, 64).

Though Raju is regarded as a 'Swami' by the villagers of Mangala and he has adjusted himself to his new role, his movement of redemption comes when he confesses to Velan that he is an imposter and an ex-convict.

It is the unshakeable faith of Velan and the villagers in Raju, which gives him the inner strength to go on with the long and arduous fast. It is also at this moment that Raju has purged himself completely of ego, falsehood, deceit and selfishness, and has become a real 'Swami.'

When Raju dissociates himself from society and pursues Rosie, he falls morally and faces unpleasant repercussions, but when he returns to society as a 'Swami' and becomes a part of it, he achieves redemption by shedding off feelings of falsehood and ego, and in the process of actually fasting pays off his arrears by penance. It becomes for him a personal moral victory because though he was only posing as a 'Swami' initially, he later earns the reverence of the people by humility, honesty, integrity and penance.

The ending of the novel is left ambiguous, perhaps deliberately—it may or may not have rained—Raju may or may not have died; but one thing is certain—there is a spiritual and moral regeneration of Raju, the guide.

Thus, it is seen that in the Western context, the individual can grow and develop, if he dissociates himself from society and becomes individualistic; whereas in the Indian context if an individual dissociates himself from society, he comes to grief, but if he takes society along with him, then he will be at peace with himself and his surroundings, and will be able to grow and develop.

REFERENCES

Emerson, R.W., "Self-Reliance." *American Literature in the Nineteenth Century: An Anthology,* Ed. William J. Fisher. New Delhi: Eurasia Publishing House, 1977.

Kakkar, Sudhir, *The Inner World: A psycho-analytic Study of Childhood and Society in India,* 1981, Delhi: OUP, 1991.

Norman Mailer, Interview, "Hip, Hell and the Navigator," *Advertisements for Myself,* 1959. London: Panther Books, 1968.

Mailer, Norman, "The White Negro." *Advertisements for Myself,* 1959.

Naik, M.K., *The Ironic Vision: A Study of the Fiction of R.K. Narayan,* New Delhi: Sterling Publishers, 1983.

Narayan, R.K., *The Bachelor of Arts,* 1937, Mysore: Indian Thought Publications, 1973.

——, *The Guide,* 1958, Mysore: Indian Thought Publications, 1975.

5

Images of Women in Bhabani Bhattacharya's Fiction

SUMAN MEHTA

Bhabani Bhattacharya is one of the pillars of Indian English fiction and has given a new direction to it. He has achieved not only national but also international fame and recognition and his works have been translated in many Indian and foreign languages. The prestigious Sahitya Academy Award of the Indian Government was awarded to him in 1967.

The works of Bhabani Bhattacharya are significant for they depict authentically the place of Indian woman in society. He presents the Indian woman as "the pure woman" in his fiction. He has presented her as a person with high ideals and a capacity for adaptability. His women characters are pure and close to nature but are invariably victimised. They are victimised by social and domestic injustice. They are full of high ideals and exuberant vitality, yet they are ultimately victimised.

Kajoli, of *So Many Hungers* (1947), is an innocent girl of fourteen. She belongs to a peasant family and lives with her brother and mother. Though this novel is basically a socio-political one, it also shows a woman being victimised. There are two plots in the novel-the story of Samarendra and his family with young Rahoul as the central figure and the story of a peasant family with a young girl Kajoli as the principal character. Devesh Babu, the grandfather of Rahoul is the joining link between the two plots. Far away from his son who lives in the city, he lives a simple life in the village with Kajoli's family.

Kajoli gets married to Kishore who is a patriot and has to leave her. Her idyllic life with Kishore is short-lived. She lives simply as a woman and is an image of joy and love. The novel deals with Bengal famine and hunger for food. Kajoli works on the farms at first but the harsh famine crushes her and her family from all sides. This hunger not only drives Kajoli and her family out of their village in search of food, but also tries to force her to sell herself. To survive she distributes bread to the destitutes of the famine affected and maintains the purity of her spirit by helping others. K.K. Sharma remarks: "Kajoli is also an incarnation of faith in the nobleness and fullness of life. She has inherited the fundamental values and manners of India, unaffected and undefiled by modern attitudes and notions."[1]

She has a deep faith in the worthiness and greatness of life. Significantly, the novelist has shown her fondness for bright and gay colours. Her keen fancy for bright colours reflects her happy and positive view of life. Rahoul's grandfather likes her very much. Speaking to Rahoul, he says, "She has a legacy of manners and proprieties to suit your new-fangled city ideas."[2]

By portraying a character like Kajoli, Bhabani Bhattacharya, affirms his positive view of life. Kajoli is his concept of ideal Indian womanhood. In the beginning of the novel, Kajoli makes a grim decision to sell her body for money, to keep her mother and younger brother alive during the famine. At such a critical moment of life, she recalls her past. She visualises her father Kanu Bhai and her husband through her mental eyes, fighting for a noble cause and dying consequently. Her eyes gleam, and she feels "a new strength in her feet and power in her spirit."[3] She decides to sell the copies of the newspaper *Hindustan* to earn money. This work makes her appear with a lovely smile on her graceful face. She helps a betel woman, who was trying to persuade her to accompany her to a harlot's house, to come back to normal life. K.K. Sharma says, "This last act is significant, as it suggests that she beats evil and moral death embodied in the betel-woman and returns to healthy life."[4]

Through the characterization of Kajoli, Bhattacharya shows the pure woman being victimised and reveals his vision of life as a compromise. It also projects his plea to present social reality in literature.

In his novel *Music for Mohini* Bhattacharya has dealt with the theme of the girl's power to adapt herself to different situations. Mohini is a charming, citybred vivacious girl. She is shown as torn between the taboos of village life and her passion for a bright and joyful life. Mohini loves life in all its colours and has a contempt for all that is dull and dead. It is hard for her to bear the images of decay. K.K. Sharma describes her thus:

> She is instinctively vivacious, playful and carefree. She loves to laugh, and needs just a slight cause to go into peals of laughter. As a young maid, she is famous for her beauty and melodious voice. When she has a longing for a lover and has really none, she does not feel very miserable. She smiles by musing on love, which is the light and saviour of life; life without love is like jasmine without scent. She lives in her dream world of romance which she creates round Somir and others. She accepts life, and does not discard it, though the eternal woman in her is dissatisfied. Even a very brief romance with a young man makes her happy.[5]

Mohini is married to Jayadev, a cold idealistic and single minded man. Her dream of a perfect happily married life is shattered and she is shocked by the behaviour of her silent, solitary husband. She is totally neglected by her husband and feels lonely. Her mother-in-law is very orthodox and traditional while she herself is modern, city-bred girl, full of new ideals, thoughts and interests. But her sister-in-law Rooplekha, suggests to her to cope with the difficulties with courage. Rooplekha is village-bred and city-wed while Mohini is city-bred and village-wed. When Rooplekha goes to the city with her husband, she has to give up her old modesty while Mohini has to traditionalize herself and adjust herself to the atmosphere of her husband's village and the Big house. In spite of unfulfilment and joylessness in her married life, she does not accept her defeat. She decides to bring happiness to her house. She is ready to accept the traditional way of life of village and her traditional mother-in-law, just for the sake of her husband. There is a mutual understanding between them at this stage. Her husband tells Mohini that she can be his Maitreyi more than a mere wife. He asks her to help him on a more dynamic path of action by taking in hand the education of the illiterate women of Behula. Mohini decides to accept the advice of her husband and feels:

> "For his sake she would absorb new ways of thought and habit, cultivate new interests. She set her mouth: life was a serious business, and she was no doll in silk and satin [...] She had duties to discharge, responsibilities. How could she let herself be defeated by discomfort and desolation."[6]

Though it was a great task, full of challenges, responsibilities and difficulties, Mohini decides that she would play her part to win the faith and favour of her husband. To be his true partner in life, she throws herself into this great task. Her hatred for her mother-in-law turns into love and she decides to let her follow her own way of life. She becomes ready to co-operate with her to offer her heart's blood in a lotus-bowl to the Virgin Goddess, so that she could bear a son. At the critical moment of this ceremonial offering, Jayadev reaches there and stops it. When Mohini finds that she was already expecting a child, she feels that her life has been fulfilled with diverse notes of music.

Other contemporary writers have shown the conflict between tradition and modernity, Bhattacharya has tried to show that with proper understanding the old and the new values can be put into harmony. He has expressed his vision through Mohini. Earlier in the novel, Bhattacharya has also shown a fierce conflict between Jayadev's mother, representing the old and superstitious and progressive people like Mohini and Jayadev. But they all enjoy harmony in their domestic life at the end of the novel due to their perfect understanding of each other. K.K. Sharma rightly observes that:

> Bhabani Bhattacharya accentuates his faith in life by showing that the opposites—the old and the new values, city life and village life, the old and the young—can live in harmony with each other. Mohini, who is city-bred, is able to develop intimacy with her old traditional mother-in-Law by virtue of her natural resilience. The result is

> happiness and peace. The clash between the old and the new modes of life, projected in the conflict between the mother of Jayadev on the one hand and Jayadev, Mohini and others on the other, disappears in the end. The two understand each other properly and there emerges a sweet harmony. When Jayadev stops his wife from performing the superstitious sacrifice to get off her barrenness under the instructions of his mother, the old woman is extremely displeased and is completely upset. But a little later after the pregnancy of Mohini, she comprehends reality with the light of reason, and the novelist bridges the gulf between the old and new.[7]

Chandralekhs, in his novel, *He Who Rides a Tiger*, is the 'moon-tinted girl,' brimming with physical vitality. She is the victim of distortion like Mohini. When her father poses as the Brahmin Mangal Adhikari and becomes the chief priest of Siva temple, Lekha too, being his daughter, is forced to perform the role of the Mother of the Seven-fold Bliss. Many people come to her from far and near expecting her to perform miracles. She adopts a little waif Obhijit, whom she has picked up from the street during the famine. She has a motherly love for him. This motherly tenderness flows in her so much that she is ready to face the wrath of the entire Brahmin crowd and to accept banishment from the temple and suffer poverty. Shantha Krishnaswamy remarks:

> At heart she is a warm hearted Bengali girl who looks forward to nothing more than a pact of companionship with Biten, the idealistic reformer, who, eschewing his, Brahmanism, was a fellow prisoner with Kalo during the famine riots in Calcutta. Her physicality as the natural woman rebels against this bogus sanctity and tries to reassert itself. One natural consequence is her out pouring of motherly love towards Obhijit, the low caste street waif she adopts.[8]

Earlier, Lekha and her father are driven to Calcutta because of hunger. Her father has been sent to jail for a while. To solve the problem of their livelihood, Lekha has been lured to a harlot house. But just at that time, her father saves her. Later on, she gains much adoration after becoming the Mother of Sevenfold Bliss. But when people come to know through Kalo's confession of the truth that they belong to the sub-caste of blacksmith's at the end of the novel, they are banished from the temple. He makes this confession because he can not see his daughter being forced to be a goddess. Lekha feels that as the harlot house had tried to corrupt her body, likewise this false divinity, imposed on her, is creating spiritual corruption within her; so, she feels a great relief when Kalo makes this confession. She and her father accept the harsh reality with grace, "and now he and Lekha, having cut themselves loose from their entanglements and deceptions, are content to begin life anew, purged of the past completely and not despairing of the future."[9]

The protagonist Meera Bai, in his novel *A Goddess Named Gold,* is a simple, large-hearted peasant girl. She had been caught in the coils of human greed for gold. The novel begins with the episode of Meera Bai's brave conduct of saving Lachmi's child, Nago, who has slipped into the well. Later on, Meera Bai becomes Meera and Lachmi becomes Lakshmi and they become the 'Cowhouse Five' along with four other women. Meera lives with her grandfather and grandmother. Her grandfather is referred to as the 'minstrel.' Meera is poised between her grandfather and Seth Samsundarji, who is Lakshmi's husband. Meera is shown as pure, brave, unselfish, unspoilt and adventurous.

Once the minstrel gives a taveez to Meera and tells her that it would prove to be a touchstone. Everytime when she performs an act of kindness, it would turn copper into gold. The innocent Meera, takes it to be real. Seth Samsunderji also thinks that the taveez really has his alchemic power. So, he makes a business deal on a fitty-fifty basis with Meera. She becomes famous as Sonamai with her touchstone. But at last, Meera casts away the taveez into the river and the minstrel tells the people that it is 'freedom,' which is the real touchstone, not the taveez.

Meera is no longer Sonamai. She is torn between her grandfather's mystic ideals and people's lust for gold. She, who is ever a compassionate mother becomes ready to give everybody in the village a gift of gold. But when her copper ornaments stay copper and no gold is forthcoming, her faith gets eroded. Then she is abused and pushed down from the pedestal of the goddess. Commenting on this, Bhattacharya remarks in the novel, "The goddess of Sonamitti, turns into the scourge of Sonamitti."[10] After this disillusionment, Meera looks forward to a bright future, full of possibilities as she has now freed herself from alien powers just like Mother India. Shantha Krishnawamy comments:

> Meera in *A Goddess Named Gold* gets down from her artificial posture as Sona Mai, the goddess of gold and desires to settle down to a peaceful life in the village under the watchful and benevolent eye of her grandfather, the wandering minstrel who is elected unanimously to the village board. Reform is definitely in the air in Sonamitti what with the minstrel and Meera the one on the village Committee and the other leading the 'Cowhouse Five', is the total woman brigade that brings colour and change to the village.'[11]

Bhattacharya's next novel, *Shadow From Ladakh,* is set against the Chinese invasion of India in 1962. The women in this novel are also victimised in one sense or the other. Bhattacharya has shown that the Gandhian principles of asceticism led women to suppress their personal desires. Suruchi was educated at Shantiniketan. There she meets Satyajit and they get married. Suruchi shares her aesthetic values with Satyajit and life becomes a sweet music for her with him. Satyajit, who had come under the influence of Tagore and Shantiniketan, now has the influence of Gandhi and Sevagram. He adopts Gandhiji's principles of asceticism.

The real problem begins, when Suruchi finds to her dismay that Satyajit has started avoiding her and their home. He feels ashamed and guilty of himself, whenever he feels attracted towards her. It is all very sad for Suruchi and she begins to feel as Meena Shirwadkar expresses it:

> "She felt she had lost her womanly dignity by this attitude of her husband. She was for life, happiness, beauty, and motherhood. She had aesthetic sense inherent in her and heightened by Tagore's Shantiniketan. But Satyajit's

> asceticism was anti-life as his friend Biresh has pointed out. He put his ideals to test at the cost of his wife's happiness. She had to suppress her wish for a son and all her womanly urges, and finally she had to allow her own daughter to be brought up in Satyajit's pattern."[12]

As a mother, she feels sorry for her daughter, Sumita, when she finds that she is caught in the same net as her father. She has a blind adoration for her father and follows his asceticism. It is very painful for her when she sees Sumita dressed like a widow and wearing no bangles. This leads her to look at Jhanak, an untouchable girl who is full of confidence and boldness. She looks beyond her home, as she discovers immense source of power within herself. She does not want to be a mere spiritual companion to her husband though she performs all her social duties at the ashram. Satyajit too thinks that she has adapted herself to the mould he had set. But Sumita perceives that there is some discontentment in her mother.

Sumita has been brought up in the small world of the ashram. She wears white dress, without kumkum or bangles. She is more conscious of the spiritual element in her than her physical desires. When she goes to Delhi, she undergoes the experience of the wider world. She finds everything new to her and she begins to evaluate her former ideals. Sumita falls in love with Bhaskar, who is a young chief-engineer trained in America. He has a very highly westernised outlook.

Bhattacharya has dealt with two modes of life in the plot of the story. They are Gandhigram and Steeltown. The Gandhigram is represented by Satayajit, who is a true follower of Gandhiji and Bhaskar represents the Steeltown. There is a fierce conflict between them as they both have totally different ideas and attitudes. Gradually the clash between them grows weaker and at last it completely disappears. Ultimately, the two different modes of life intermingle with each other. This synthesis is significant as it denotes the understanding between Bhaskar and Suruchi. Now everybody has overcome his or her conflict and frustration. Satyajit is happier than ever before as he now feels that only the fusion of conflicting values and modes of life can bring a joyful and happy life. Suruchi, who has forgotten the aesthetic way of life of love and beauty, seems to live a real life again. Bhaskar who has been upset by his sense of alienation for a long time, gets rid of it and Sumita who has suppressed her natural instincts, is full of joy and happiness of life. She is able to bring a harmonious compromise between Gandhigram and Steeltown, between ascetic and aesthetic way of life and the old and new values of love and duty. Meena Shirwadkar states:

> In the end, both the women not only come out of the Gandhian or rather the ascetic principles of Satyajit but go beyond it to blend the ascetic and the aesthetic (Gandhi and Tagore) ways of life, or Gandhigram and Steeltown (Gandhi and Nehru), the spinning wheel and the turbine (East and West). Women in this novel serve to bring about social harmony.[13]

Bhabani Bhattacharya shows that his characters, both male and female have a positive attitude towards life. Sumita, at the end of the novel, freed herself from her father's power and some of the asceticism, finds life's true fulfilment in the true and spontaneous love, which now overflows in her.

One more female character in the same novel is Rupa, who is half American and half Indian. She is a beautiful girl but epitomises the cross cultural conflicts. Shantha Krishnaswamy thinks, "We have Rupa and Bhaskar in *Shadow From Ladakh*, mutually attracted and yet destroying each other everytime they are thrown together. It is Rupa who emerges the victim: to preserve her sanity, she decides to flee Steeltown. Bhaskar has the regenerative umbrella of Sumita; Rupa has no such protective mantle."[14] Rupa, being disappointed and broken-hearted in her first love, gives up her job of an air-hostess. She keeps herself buried in a hotel room sealed up and then, as Bhattacharya has put it, "a new Rupa emerged out of her chastened self."[15]

In his woman protagonists, Bhattacharya often sees a woman as a mother. He is of the view that a woman is capable of great heroic deeds and self denial in her role as a mother. He thinks that motherhood is something beyond this world. She is the giver and protector of life. She willingly carries the burden of the sins of her children. The mother in *So Many Hungers* is an embodiment of compassion, sacrifice, unselfishness, strength and hope. Kajoli's mother is not only a mother in their family, but she is the mother of the whole village. She, who is not ready to sell her cow, even in their days of starvation, readily gives her cow to a woman who has no milk for her dying baby.

The woman, as mother in Bhattacharya's fiction, has her own path of duty cut out for her. She is linked with the usual vision of gentleness and nurture. She gains and suffers as a mother. Bhattacharya has expressed his unshakable, faith in motherhood. Mohini in *Music for Mohini* was famous as the Little Mother of the village. Chandralekha in *He Who Rides a Tiger* was adorned as the mother of Sevenfold bliss. She looks after Obhijit with motherly tenderness. Meera becomes Sonamai in *A Goddess Named Gold* with her touchstone.

Bhabani Bhattacharya has shown motherhood as a protective force and upholder of traditional values. He has portrayed her as a suffering figure. He has also shown that a woman, as a mother is strong enough, as far as her children's protection is concerned. He has projected his vision of life not only in older mothers but in young mothers too. Commenting on his woman characters, Shantha Krishnaswamy writes:

> Bhabani Bhattacharya creates the woman protagonist as a finer human instrument than the male. She is wondrous, light, ethereal being filled with radiance, with possibilities. She is pure in the sense that she is close to nature as in tune with her instinctual urges. She is also pure in the sense that she is filled with noble ideals. Through her, the author aims at interlinking polarities, at connecting culture with culture, tradition with modernity, the individual and society.[16]

Unlike other contemporary writers, Bhabani Bhattacharya has presented the Indian woman as the pure woman in his novels, who has been victimised inspite of her high ideals and vitality. This concept of the innocent victimised Indian woman is a constant feature of his novels. He has also created some woman protagonists in his novels. They are full of noble ideas, which are more refined than those of their male counterparts. He has effectively portrayed the role of motherhood in his fiction. He feels that a woman in her capacity as a mother is capable of great deeds. As a mother, she is a symbol of gentleness, love and sacrifice. He shows that the woman as a wife is also human and is an equal partner of man. Most of his heroines are pure and simple.

Bhattacharya has dealt with both rustic and urban female characters in his fiction. They all belong to the middle class families. Bhattacharya has presented his woman characters as the victims of evil-ridden society, of ignorance, stoic suffering and sacrifice. But he does not fail to show a rapid change in the position of woman in India. He shows that she is not crushed all the time. She looks forward and finds the world full of opportunities. Prof. R.S. Singh remarks, "The psychology of the maturing girls and the imperceptibly changing attitude of the parents towards them are delineated by Bhattacharya with tenderness and care."[17]

The women in Bhattacharya's fiction play the role of a connector and link between tradition and modernity, between Eastern and Western way of living, between the city life and village life and between idealism and spiritualism. They create harmony wherever they go. Though they may be victimised, they are ready to face the future with confidence at the end of the novel. He affirms that women can play a positive role in the development of society by projecting optimistic and affirmative pictures of Indian woman. Bhattacharya has dealt with different kinds of women characters in his novels. He has presented pure women who try hard as a wife, beloved and mother, yet are victimised. He shows his faith in the power of women as a redeemer. His women protagonists serve as a link between themselves and their country. They are full of confidence and look forward hopefully for a better life. Shantha Krishnaswamy feels, "He affirms again and again that the woman need not be a victim; she can play a positive role in the development of society."[18]

NOTES

1. K.K. Sharma, *Bhabani Bhattacharya: His Vision and Themes* (New Delhi: Abhinav Publications, 1979), 17.

2. Bhabani Bhattacharya, *So Many Hungers* (Mumbai, Jaico Publishing House, 1964), 25.
3. *So Many Hungers*, 207.
4. Sharma, 25.
5. Sharma, 26-27.
6. Bhabani Bhattacharya, *Music For Mohini* (New Delhi: An Orient Paperback, 1952), 105-106.
7. Sharma, 28.
8. Shantha Krishnawamy, *The Woman in Indian Fiction in English* (New Delhi: Ashish Publishing House, 1984), 69.
9. K.R.S. Iyenger, *Indian Writing in English* (New Delhi: Sterling Publishers Pvt. Ltd., 1962), 418.
10. Bhabani Bhattacharya, *A Goddess Named Gold* (New Delhi: Hind Pocket Books Pvt. Ltd., 1960), 224.
11. Krishnaswamy, 64.
12. Meena Shirwadkar, *Image of Woman in the Indo-Anglian Novel* (New Delhi: Sterling Publishers Pvt. Ltd., 1979), 123.
13. Shirwadkar, 125.
14. Krishnaswamy, 75.
15. Bhabani Bhattacharya, *Shadow from Ladakh* (New Delhi: Hind Pocket Books pvt. Ltd., 1966), 135.
16. Krishnaswamy, 61-62.
17. *Indian Novel in English: A Critical Study* (New Delhi: Arnold—Heinemann, 1976), 32.
18. Krishnaswamy, 81.

6

An Analysis of Kamala Das's *Padmavati The Harlot and Other Stories*

JOYA CHAKRAVARTY

Kamala Das is the new feminist voice in Indian Literature voicing forth a woman's point of view. She represents the sensibility and sensitivity of the modern Indian woman. Kamala Das has been hailed as the 'new woman' of Indian writing in English. She broke away from all irrational customs and conventions of society. In *Padmavati The Harlot and Other Stories* the women characters are aware of their rights and privileges; they have an independence and identity of their own and they are defiant of the hitherto accepted ritualistic traditions.

Kamala Das is a bilingual poet from Kerala. She began writing poems in her very childhood. The anti-traditional themes of her poems and short stories challenged the foundations of Indian society and helped to re-define the sphere of Indian Women's writings.

The women characters in this collection have a majestic aura about them even though they give in to men. In the story 'That Woman' the woman has a very calm and dignified air about her. Her lover is dead—She must begin her life again—life must go on: "there is nothing of mine remaining here"—saying this she goes out of the house without a backward glance. She does not wish to claim anything, she does not wish to harass the man's wife and children—there is within her a resoluteness of purpose, a dignity in the face of adversity.

The stories in this collection are very different from those of the patriarchal Indian canon and pushes readers to attend to texts that are not inscribed in conventionally literary language. Domestic language often seems invisible to those who have not learned to read it. Kamala Das breaks through the rigidity of the Indian Literacy Tradition, one which reified patriarchal control and tradition built upon it. Kamala Das breaks away from the stereotyped images of women, images which have strait jacketed the very thought process and behaviour of women. Her stories have generated forms and continuities very different from traditional stories. Take for instance the story "Sanatan Choudhuri's wife." In her sleep Gopi Menon's wife murmur's the name of Sanatan and Gopi begins to have doubts about his wife's fidelity. He decides to put her to test and one day he returns without taking the train to his place of work. He follows his wife to a house and finds her in the company of an elderly man. Gopi is aggrieved—he knocks on the door of the house and tells the servant that he has come to see the master. Subsequently he meets Mr Chaudhuri and his wife Mrinalini. Gopi notes Mrinalini's striking resemblance to Mrs Gopi Menon—the same features, the same Audrey Hepburn smile. Who is she? Is she Mrs Menon or Mrs Chaudhuri? It is interesting to note what the word "Sanatan" means—eternal—it can symbolise the eternal male expectations and attitudes towards women. Between the elderly Mr Chaudhuri and the young Gopi Menon is this woman. The reference to Audrey Hepburn who is a well known actress shows that a woman can switch to different roles—but there has been no significant attitudinal change in men. The new woman has arrived—where is the new man?

Kamala Das's stories are ambiguous and they can be interpreted in more than one way. But no two interpretations converge. There is creativity in her work no doubt but the reader is not prepared for these sudden twists and turns. The unexpectedness of her writings, her fearless exposure of the so-called untalked of themes speaks volumes for her capacity.

Kamala Das's prose is succinct and suggestive and the reader has no difficulty in following it. Take for instance, the story "Iqbal" (53). A pregnant woman is intrigued by her husband's unusual fascination for a young boy. It is a homosexual association but Kamala Das does not explore this theme apart from hinting at it. Instead Mrs Das focuses on the femininity of the woman: sensing Iqbal's jealousy due to the sterile homosexual relationship, the woman laughs as if rejoicing in her creativity. The laughter rings in the corridors of the hospital where Iqbal is recovering after an attempt at suicide. It is interesting to note that the woman is not perturbed and neither is she disturbed. By laughing at Iqbal, she dismisses him and his associations with her husband and asserts her supremacy, her ability to handle her problems.

In *Padmavati, The Harlot and Other Stories,* Kamala Das appears to champion the cause of the underprivilege women. The prostitutes in these stories give in generously—the wives may sulk, may proclaim their rights and privileges—but the prostitutes give off their bodies generously without being demanding. The prostitutes abide by the men—yet there is within them a casualness, a disinterestedness and they assert their supremacy by retaining their individuality. The prostitutes fill the vacuum that is there in the lives of the men. Man is seen as son, lover and God and the woman is in quest of satisfaction. Even when the woman surrenders she acquires a dignity because of her inner awareness of her selfhood.

In the title story, "Padmavati the Harlot," Padmavati comes to pay homage at the temple. She is late and the temple is closed so the loafers loitering near the shrine tease her. Her offerings are snatched away by these loafers. Undaunted Padmavati enters the temple yard and knocks at the door of the temple. The door opens. She does not look up, she only sees the bejewelled toes and confesses about her life. She has nothing to offer him. She says, "If you were a man I would have given you my body, stale and ageing, but you are a God. What can I give you?

She felt the warmth of His body against her own. She closed her eyes in ecstasy. At dawn, she left the precincts of the shrine and walked down the steps with her hair dishevelled and her blouse torn in places. She blushed like a bride when the young men at the foot of the hill came near her and looked at her face.

There were bruises on her cheeks and on her white throat. Her lips were swollen and blue. There was fatigue in her eyes. She hid her face behind her long hair and walked fast. The young men let her pass, bowing before her and murmuring "Mother, go in safety, give us your blessings and go your way [...]."

In Kamala Das no one interpretation can be taken as final. Padmavati, a mere prostitute, has been accepted by the Lord and He has forgiven her. Kamala Das was well aware of the Devadasi system and in this story there is an indication that this system is still prevalent. Then again we are all aware of the 'Nagar Bodu' system—Amrapalli is a striking example—the Nagar Bodu was proud of her status. But in this story when Padmavati goes away she hides her face—this shame and shyness in one who has been considered to be shameless by society is an indication that even such women have feelings and they who provide solace to others, also feel the need to be taken care of.

Kamala Das's works probe the complex human activities through which many women have shaped their lives and within which they have discovered their powers, limits, restrictions and connections as females and as human beings. In speaking of the capacious and problematic oeuvres of her characters, Kamala Das notes that they have achieved some standing despite their attention to the domestic sphere.

WORK CITED

1. Chaudhari, Indra Nath, Comparative Indian Literature, Some perspectives, New Delhi: Sterling Publishers, 1992.
2. Das, Kamala, Padmavati the Harlot and Other Stories New Delhi: Sterling Publishers, 1992.
3. Dhawan R.K., Indian Women Novelists, New Delhi: Prestige Books, 1991.
4. Iyengar, K.R.S., Indian writing in English, New Delhi: Sterling Publishers, 1983.
5. Shirwadkar, Meena, Image of Women in the Indo-Anglican Novel, New Delhi: Sterling Publishers, 1979.

7

Fair Treatment to the Fair Sex

NISHI UPADHYAYA

In a male-dominated hegemony of patriarchal ideology the position of a woman is precarious. Down the ages women are compelled to live in a society which recognises only men as primary existents and women as auxiliaries. The present paper is a psychological study of man-woman relationship in two short stories—"Stench of Kerosene" by Amrita Pritam and "Lajwanti" by Rajinder Singh Bedi. In both the stories women suffer for no fault of their own.

Amrita Pritam, being a woman herself, is acutely conscious of the imbalance in the man-woman relationship and it is a theme recurrent in her fiction. In the story "Stench of Kerosene" the man, Manek, forsakes his wife Guleri, on the behest of his mother because she has not been able to give him an offspring in the last seven years of their marital life. An ideal woman's duty was to give herself up to the care of others, to work self-effacingly to further the interest and honour of man and to procreate. Since Guleri fails in one of her duties she is abandoned. A deeper psychological analysis reveals the fact that Guleri suffers not because her husband is strong and powerful but because of the inherent weakness of her husband. In the heart of his hearts Manek does not want Guleri to go to her parents place this year because he is aware of the fact that his mother has made arrangements for his second marriage in Guleri's absence. Not only is he unable to reveal the fact to Guleri but he is also unable to oppose his mother. He does not have the courage to protect the rights and honour of his wife.

"Obedient to his mother and to custom Manek's body responded to the new woman."[1] Manek is not bold enough even to fight for his own happiness. "But his heart was dead within him."[2] The news of Guleri committing suicide by soaking her clothes in kerosene and setting fire to them makes him guilty-conscious. "He was like a man dead, his face quite blank, his eyes empty."[3] He is guilt-ridden to the extent that when his mother, after bathing his son and dressing him in fine clothes, puts him in Manek's lap, the boy to Manek stinks of kerosene. Just like Lady Macbeth, Manek's pricks of conscience makes it impossible for him to forget the injustice done to Guleri. The result of that injustice is his son and he seems to stink of kerosene.

The story Lajwanti by Rajinder Singh Bedi is based on the theme of Ramayana. Sunderlal's wife, Lajwanti, has been abducted during the partition riots. To rehabilitate the recovered abducted women a "Rehabilitation of Hearts" Committee is set up and Babu Sunderlal is elected its Secretary. The slogan of the supporters is, "Rehabilitate them in your hearts." It's after losing Lajwanti that Sunderlal realizes how badly he had behaved with Lajwanti during their married life. "[...] he had allowed himself to be irritated with everything she did—even with the way she stood up or sat down, the way she cooked and the way she served his food; he had thrashed her at every pretext."[4] Wife-beating was a common tendency in all classes of men, high or low. Husbands used to humiliate and make their wives feel worthless. Submission to male authority in a cheerful and humble manner was high on the list of feminine virtues, and their passivity, an applauded quality.

Now Sunderlal pledges that if he is given another chance he would really rehabilitate Lajwanti in his heart and set an example to the people. He felt that these poor women were not to be blamed as they were victimised by lecherous ravishers and a society which refuses to accept these helpless women is rotten beyond redemption and deserves to be liquidated.

As a part of his rehabilitation movement Sunderlal raises his voice against Shri Ram Chandra banishing his wife, Sita, on the remark of a poor washerman. According to Sunderlal innocent Sita was the victim of the wickedness of Ravans and then the injustice of Shri Ram Chandra. Finally, one day Sunderlal is informed by Lalchand that he had seen Lajwanti on the border at Wagah. "The chillum fell from Sunderlal's hand; the sweetened tobacco scattered on the floor."[5] Initially he is not ready to accept the news. "It must have been someone else [...]."[6] When Lalchand correctly describes all the tattoo marks on Lajwanti's body Sunderlal has to accept the news.

Now, the facade built up by Sunderlal falls down. Contrary to all his preachings he becomes "nervous and could not make up his mind whether to go to meet her or wait for her at home."[7] All he wanted to do now was, "to run away; to spread out all the banners and placards he had carried, sit in their midst and cry to his heart's content."[8] But now Sunderlal cannot escape from the movement started by him. So finally, he and Lajwanti proceed to their home amidst slogans and speeches. Paradoxically, Sunderlal is unable to accept his wife on an equal footing. He deifies her. "[...] he had installed a living idol in his inner most sanctum and sat outside the gate like a sentry."[9] He starts addressing her as goddess-devi. For Sunderlal, Lajwanti is no longer a woman of flesh and blood but only a means of salvation for him. Sunderlal deals with her with utmost care and their relationship becomes devoid of any human touch of intimacy.

Lajwanti longs for Sunderlal to become "the same old Sunderlal with whom she quarrelled over a carrot and who appeased her with a radish."[10] But there is not a chance of quarrel. Lajwanti has been "rehabilitated" but not accepted. This is the crux of the story.

The urge of the woman to be accepted by man on an equal footing wholeheartedly is evident in both the stories. In the first story the man succumbs to the domestic pressure and totally abandons his wife. In the second story, the man succumbs to the pressure from the society and brings his wife back home but he does not accept her wholeheartedly. Their relationship lacks warmth and total involvement. Both the men lack courage, compassion and generosity. Man and woman can work on a collaborative basis and lead better lives. Man-woman relationship will be profoundly altered, for the better, if their relations are based on an equal footing.

REFERENCES

1. Amrita Pritam, *Stench of Kerosene* translated by Khuswant Singh, *Contemporary Indian Short Stories* edited by Ka Naa Subramanyam, Vikas Publishing House Pvt. Ltd., 1977, 121.
2. *Ibid.*, 121.
3. *Ibid.*, 122.
4. Rajinder Singh Bedi, *Lajwanti* translated by Khuswant Singh, *Contemporary Indian Short Stories* edited by Ka Naa Subramanyam, Vikas Publishing House Pvt. Ltd., 1977, 142.
5. *Ibid.*, 148.
6. *Ibid.*, 148.
7. *Ibid.*, 149.
8. *Ibid.*, 149-150.
9. *Ibid.*, 151.
10. *Ibid.*, 152.

8

How Difficult it was to be Backhome! Vikram Seth's *From Heaven Lake Travels Through Sinkiang and Tibet*

SURESH K. SHUKLA

Mr Seth's travelogue *From Heaven Lake Travels Through Sinkiang and Tibet* runs into nineteen uneven chapters. It can be broadly divided into three sections: China, Tibet, Nepal and back home. Mr Seth [...] as the protagonist does not follow any conventional approach. However, an avid reader can guess that he might have spent less than three months in this journey. Mr Seth begins his touring to the most (Turfan) remote part of China, Turfan in the month of July and ends it by the third week of August; year is not mentioned.

As one of the students of the Nanjing University, Mr Seth found a chance to visit Turfan [...]

'Fire Place' [...] the tombs of Qin Shi, the first great 'Unifier' of China, and the Empress of Ming Huang and the grand mosque of Xiang. His visits are mainly in extreme climatic situations. Turfan [...] a place wherein one can cook an egg in the sand, as temperature is on normal summer day 45°C. The town lives in the dappled shade of its vines. Trellises span everything, including most of the streets, it is a place for indolents, where whole families sleep out-doors, heaped together on antique bed steads. Liuyuan is on the periphery which is known as the Black-Gobi. Mr Seth points out that the Chinese have ruled it fitfully for centuries. Its native inhabitants are Muslim and Turkish people, the protagonist's undertone is that the recent

Chinese settlers seem ill at ease with the harsh immensity of the landscape and the uncouth enthusiasm of the local people.

In spite of the impact of the pacification in China, there are traces of religious temperaments especially among the minority Muslims. Apparently, there is a heavy grip of the Red Guards in every nook and corner of China and Tibet too. Mr Seth [...] as an adventurer, takes pleasure in every manifestation of strange, beautiful and unpleasant experience. It is true that travelling broadens one's mind, one might cultivate a sense of adaptability and strengthen sociability too. Mr Seth impresses us as a hardy youth who could match with the moment, be it sharing of eatables or puffing a Chinese bidi; he would never pose himself as a fastidious fellow. His narration is not very systematic; probably throughout his journey there is an element of uncertainty as he travels from one place to the other. There might be innumerable empty days or a day of boredom but he keeps up patience and perseverance to face all oddities. On the way to Lhasa from Liuyuan, his big black bag full of books and research materials had slipped off the van. Thus, it can be considered one of the most unforgettable experiences, fortunately the Chinese police could oblige him with his safe return. An avid reader of this travelogue would trace Vikram's little discomfort and problem of adjustment through striking statements. One statement reads as:

> [...] 'I do not think that I will be able to tolerate the limitations of group travel' (6).

On reading this book, there is hardly anything like discontent or lurking enviousness in Mr Vikram, in fact, the traveller's voyage might not be very nauseating but quite confusing. Even the villages are a few and far between. On several occasions, there is an attempt to give a great variety of word pictures which definitely sustain general reader's interest. These are mainly about 'Heaven Lake, the South Lake Nanhu, the Emin minaret and a ceremony near the Sara monastery [...] LHASA. It reads as:

(a) [...] 'Heaven-Lake' is long, sardine shaped and fed by snowmelt from a stream at its head. The lake is intense blue, surrounded on all sides by green mountains, walls dotted with distant sheep. At the head of the lake, beyond the delta of the in-flowing stream, is a massive snow-capped peak which dominate the vista, it is a part of series of peaks that culminate, a little out of view, in Mountain Bogda itself' (22).

On seeing the bluish water, Mr Seth was tempted to dive into it but Mr Caos [...] the hotel—keeper's timely advice stopped him in doing so. It was because of an accidental death of an athlete from Beijing.

(b) [...] The desert sky is abruptly dark, and a huge gust of wind sweeps, the dust of the street into swivelling and blinding haze. A great thunder clap follows, and rain pours down. When the haze settles I see cobblers and tailors vanish (42).

On the edge of the Oasis of Turfan (Turfan!) lie, Goachang and Joache lie ruined cities; probably Mr Seth fails to record his impression about them. It dates from the heyday of the Silk Road. The walls of Bezeklin with innumerable caves has a river gorge quite high in the mountains not far away. These caves are stuffed with colourful and flamboyant paintings rich in Persian, Chinese, Indian and Turkish influences. The Emin minaret is a fantastically decorated mud-brick tower quite adjacent to a mosque of simple geometry by which Mr Seth seems to be not much impressed. However, Mr Seth remarks:

> 'Emin Tower a tall phallus of clay whose shifting shadow falls on fields and around [...]' (16).

At one stage, Mr Seth gives a vivid description of the most dreadful ceremony near the Sera monastery, Lhasa. It reads as:

> '[...] these are human corpses lying on the rock, stripped and held in place by the head, while the lower torso, beginning from the legs is hacked or cut up.'

The eagles sweep down from the ridge and wheel in huge dark circles, lower and lower, finally, settling on a small hill near the rock (148).

Thus, Mr Seth narrates stupidities, tortures and brutalities witnessed. It is made even more real by the equally cool and objective references to subjects normally the Chinese as well as the Tibetan social taboos.

It cannot be any secret that the Chinese might have occupied and lived far and wide, making a permanent imprint even on the very roof [...] of the Global World [...] Tibet. It is definitely an approach of a carnivorus giant. Of course, Mr Seth does not make any statement about the Geo-political standards of the present day China, Tibet or Nepal.

In the middle of this book, Mr Seth, as a lonely traveller remains always alert to start or to break his journey. There is no trace of any regret about untimely breaks; probably he might have enjoyed even aesthetically. Thus, *From Heaven Lake Travels Through Sinkiang and Tibet* is an interesting travelogue with good deal of information about China and Tibet. Mr Seth offers no judgements about the places visited, however, there is conscientiously, an effort to sustain the reader's interest.

Nevertheless, Mr Seth gives the reader a feel of the burning sense of injustice, be it a situation wherein a young lama is seen continuously chanting, Om Mai Padma Hum or a young Chinese bogged down in routine sheepish life and keeps on saying 'Ta-ma-de' *i.e.*, the Chinese swearing. A reader would definitely admire Mr Seth's sociability with Mr John, Abdurrahamah, a guide, Mr Sui, a truck driver, Mr Quazha a public security officer, Mr Guyansang a Tibetan. There are some striking observations not only about the Chinese liking for 'Raj and Rita' of 'Awara' (Raj Kapoor and Nargis) but also for 'funny money and the presence of foreigner [...] Waigoren Waiben [...] Waiben (*i.e.*, Out-land persons [...] foreign guest).

According to Mr Seth the status of a foreign friend or foreign guest in China is interesting. Even the elite Chinese would never hesitate to say [...]

'We have friends all over the world [...]' However, if there is an affair of a foreigner, especially with the fair sex, they might feel horrified. Mr Seth is full of praise about train journeys in China, probably he speaks from his experience of travelling from Liuyuan to Lhasa; similarly he does not connive with the present day set-up of the Chinese society. To illustrate it clearly.

> [...] the viciousness of the Cultural revolution during which they were encouraged to turn against their parents and teachers and every one in authority, and instead to follow

> the (prevailing) message of Mao. All decency died, during that time, he says, half the cultural heritage of China books, temples, works of art was destroyed (176).

It is a fact that people's protests are overruled by the Chinese authority with a smile. Potala...once the place of His Excellency Dalai Lama has turned out to be a prison for the Tibetans. Even by the fag end of this book, Mr Seth keeps an eye on nature, even though his short stay at Nilamu might be for a few hours. Once again, he describes a waterfall.

> [...] and across the grey vertically of a cliff a thin strand of water indeed vanishes into a mist or smoke atomised by the wind, to reappear, reconstituted from it seems the air itself into a liquid skin of light. There is enchantment in flowing water, I sit hypnotised by its beauty the water, the most unifying of the elements, that links land and sea and air in one living ring, it has a channelled flow, unlike air, and its cycles are vaster, accepting all three states in nature (165).

Thus, Mr Seth is very well aware of the world climatic zones which are arranged in latitudinal bands. Finally, he is running up the race to end his journey; he says:

> [...] I am in a rapid southwards descent to the warm foot hills of the Indian sub continent [...] (163).

Towards the end Vikram Seth draws a brief but strong contrast between India and China's implementation of the family planning, child-care and even about the law and order situation in general. Corruption, racialism and slum landlordism do excite the young Chinese as well as Indians. Lastly, the author is revealed as perhaps at least a young Indian wizard who claims to be well aware of way of life in China, Tibet, Nepal and India too.

REFERENCES

1. *From Heaven Lake Travels Through Sinkiang and Tibet* (Penguin Books, India), 1990 by Mr Vikram Seth.
2. *Changing Chinese Society* by CH'U CHAI & Winberg Chai A Mentor Book (The New American Library).

9

Confronting Modernity and Post-Coloniality: *The Last Burden* and *English, August: An Indian Story*

NAMRATHA MOGARAL

There seems to be a major reappraisal of the term modernity in recent fiction in English in India. In an earlier decade, as for Mulk Raj Anand, modernity meant social emancipation and progress, very often linked with technological and material issues. The narrative style was realistic and straightforward; the characters were strong and they conversed with each other or just. sloganeered.

But in recent times there has been the rise of the 'urban novel' which has all the ingredients of high modernist style and preoccupations—concern for one's roots, feeling of alienation and ennui, preoccupation with sexuality, pull of the city and its corruption, so on. In addition, an unrelenting satirical gaze at contemporary India prevails and a desire to reconcile with its fractured past is strident in ways that obscures its connection with the freedom struggle—which is a main source of inspiration for earlier novelists—but not with India's status as a post-colonial nation.

Upamanyu Chatterjee is the most representative writer of the 'urban novel'. For one, both the novels he has written reveal anxiety about the modern Indian identity. There is also concern for rediscovering one's cultural roots and past and to come to terms with the post-colonial status. Taken together, *The Last Burden* (1993) and *English, August: An Indian Story* (1988) gives an account of the geneology of modern Indian sensibility: its roots in modern domesticity and proliferation via bureaucracy.

While *The Last Burden* is overtly concerned with presenting women's role as wife, sexual slave and vassal and the bondage of family ties, the under text is that of the Indian family slowly breaking up in a modern milieu. In the character of Jamun and Burfi, Chatterjee depicts the slow erosion of the Indian family mores by Christianity and English education, tolls of capitalism and urbanisation and the middle class status it bestows.

It is ironical that Urmila and Shyamanand, Jamun and Burfi's parents are married in the fateful year of 1950—the year India became a republic with its own constitution. They are representative of first-generation post-independence Indians who believe in the values of the West as modernity, give their children English education and encourage them to cultivate Western friends. So much so both children and parents quote the Bible for domestic wisdom rather than the Hindu scriptures. Perhaps, Chatterjee intends sarcasm here that the modern family draws more from Bible than any other for sustenance and justification. Since "the wise men of old" (Upanishads) did not advocate raising a family: "what should we do with children," they said "when we have Brahman and the world besides" (103). Of course, Chatterjee does not always endorse such philosophical resignation.

Moreover, they have exchanged their roots, patriarchal land has been sold off, for money. Shyamanand is a creature of modern capitalism as Chatterjee satirizes "[...] to mothball the interest on a fixed deposit—never to wade into it—with that interest after months to archly open a Recurring Deposit, and with the interest of the Recurring Deposit to start some term deposit, or national savings—like playing trader or monopoly" (64).

'Needless to say, they are thoroughly urban, Shyamanand's job requiring them to change cities frequently, a cactus being the only continuity in their lives. They have long shunned living in an extended family and are a microcosm in the truly western sense, a self-contained nucleus against the world that intrudes only in the form of ayahs.

Burfi wedded to a Christian wife "modernity dribbling out of her boobs" (103), in the end longs to have had stronger roots in Hindu philosophy and blames his parents for it, even as his father realizes that inspite of his modern ambitions for his sons, he never intended them to be such "Grammy Sugars." This volte-face is true of other characters in the novel, Kasturi, Jamun etc. The shifting meaning of modernity is acknowledged.

In an almost Woolfsain narrative, with sometimes Eliotian twang, that places it squarely among the modernists *The Last Burden* slowly deconstructs the domestic roots of modern India. The *English August: An Indian Story* on the other hand directly confronts modernity and nationalism in the contemporary Indian context on a public plane. A picaresque burdened by a colonial past, the novel is unable to extricate the 'seeking self' from issues of nationality and modernity.

Yet, Agastya the satirical quest-hero does not belong to the Gandhian or even the Nehruvian era. These names do not signify anything to him. His initial vision of India is of "Scores of people, sitting on their haunches, smoking, wandering, gazing at anything moving or at other people. Most were in dhoti, kurta and Gandhi cap (or was it Nehru cap? wondered Agastya No, Gandhi cap and Nehru Jacket. Or Gandhi jacket and Nehru cap? And Patel vest? And Mountbatten lungi and Rajaji shawl and Tagore dhoti?), Some had towels over their heads [...]" (11). He is a late twentieth century 'yuppie' clad in jeans and baggy shirt, smoking pot while he listens to Ella Fitzerald and Vivaidly. His roots in the freedom struggle and its nationalism are not strong, but then neither is it relevent to relive them. He is the new-generation Indian who has to discover his freedom all over again.

Moreover, national identity for him is not of dichotomous opposition between himself and the colonizers, as it would have been in pre-independent India but of India *versus* a disparate world of "Time-Life" and Coco cola and Calvin Klen jeans and T-shirts. Neither is there 'unity' within the Indian identity, which was a key sensibility that shaped the spirit of nationalism in pre-independent India, he realizes "Agastya looked at him and thought, too many worlds, concentric and he a restless centre. Madna, and within it Jompana, Chopanthi, Goropak, Mariagarh, like names out of magic, strong with an idiosyncratic tang, still reeking of the tribals that had once been their only inhabitants. And the megapolitan world of Delhi and Calcutta, the bewitching, become elusive, alternative beyond which was the hinterland that countless trains tore through every day, with its dots of Ratlam and Azamganj. And stretching out to the infinite was the Time-Life world, from which John Avery had come, to which Dhrubo's Renu had gone, only to feel dislocated" (218). Thus his India is diverse and contradictory.

He seeks to belong to the class of elite, the IAS which again has origins in the colonial past. The IAS and its bureaucratic processes is also the proliferating grid of modernity. Except people like Ramana Karanth who runs a leper home few can escape its ordering and naming tantacles. English, radio and TV become its insidious means of influence that captures even the rural and tribals of Madna, Jampanna or Chipanthi.

Agastya finds himself burdened by more than one past, the colonial which makes him want to be Anglo, the traditional Indian which turns him again and again to the traditional wisdom of Hindu philosophy of the *Bhagvadgita* and Gandhi. Somehow, since the colonial legacy also means modernity and change it becomes difficult for the satirical hero to shake it off and embrace tradition totally.

He is unable to achieve the untroubled synthesis of nationalism and modernity that his father, governor of Calcutta, clad in silk-kurta dhoti, eating corned beef and encouraging an English education, has reached. Moreover, his uncle Manik is also progressive, wanting his daughter to have an English education so that she can have an edge over the rest of Indians. Pultukaku uses his obscure American treatise on third-world journalism.

This attitude towards modernity as embodied in an English education and western outlook on life is proved inadequate in the modern Indian cultural situation. The inability to sever the deep roots of Indian culture and tradition is exposed.

The traditional past is not merely ornamental in form of a few temples and tourist curios but an active force that works despite oneself. This Agastya discovers for himself, despite his juvenile ambitions of becoming an Anglo, craving to be called August instead of Agastya. He is attracted to Shankar who is dedicated to thumri music, and Sathe to his cartoons. Both, despite having no pretensions to elitism or high-brow art are Indian in sensibility. Or even Tamse who has attempted to evolve a modern Indian imagination. Chatterjee even sees in these debauched artists a proto-type for a modern Indian culture, a synthesis of all the fractured parts of the Indian sensibility; the orthodox past, the colonial experience and the modern post-independent India.

Despite the satirical gaze at modern rural India, it has its highlights. Chatterjee, in modern India sees the true resolution of India's traditional heritage and philosophy and modernity. The tribal woman Para, who boldly comes to Agastya about the village well but who sits behind Rajan the naxalite is the modern Bhavani or Durga or Jagadamba as Shankar, Vasant and Agastya of the city call the Goddess. Neera who light-heartedly loses her virginity again is like Para striving to come out of orthodox gender matrixes laid down by a male-hegemonic past.

In Chatterjee's modern India the disruptive, and to a certain extent subversive, forces of fascism that these women associate with draw inspiration from the same source of wisdom of magic and myth that has hitherto marked off some obscure source of sustenance as the pool at Gorapak, beyond Madna.

The concrete narrative with authentic descriptions of rural and urban life presents a multitudinous India in a pastiche, each bit highlighting the other in contradiction and struggles to come to terms with modernity. It is Agastya's satirical gaze, like Srivastav the District collector's scowling face that keeps the narrative always on the other side of jingoism. Agastya's philosophical skepticism makes him comparable with the Indian philosopher symbolized by "Dadru" the frog (which in Hindu mythology stands for the skeptical intellectual) in his bathroom.

A rapturous passage describing Delhi and Calcutta at dusk (144-145) evokes Eliot and Joyce's description of the city and contrasts with the squalor of rural India and places Chatterjee in the tradition of moderns, celebrating the modern urban consciousness. Inspite of seeking succour in Indian tradition and culture there is no atavistic longing for the pastoral.

REFERENCES

Chatterjee, Upamanyu, *English, August: An Indian Story,* Rupa: New Delhi, 1988.

Chatterjee, Upamanyu, *The Last Burden,* Viking: New Delhi, 1993.

Kumar, Sukrita Paul, *Conversations on Modernism,* Indian Institute of Advanced Studies: Shimla, 1990.

Sarma, Gobinda Prasad *Nationalism in India Anglîcan Fiction,* Sterling: New Delhi, 1990.

Singh, Avadesh K. (ed.), *Contemporary Indian Fiction in English,* Creative Books: New Delhi, 1993.

10

The Demon of Debt: Mukul Kesavan's *Looking Through Glass*

NANDINI NAYAR

[...] because she had paid my dues.

—Mukul Kesavan, *Looking Through Glass*

Looking Through Glass (1995)[1], Mukul Kesavan's debut (and so far only) novel, teems with personal balance sheets of its characters. Dues that require payment and references to the "economic" aspect of life constitute the very "parlance" of the novel. The nature of the dues varies with every character. While Ammi labours under a purely imaginary debt (her demon), Dadi has to contend with the debt she owes her country. Masroor is driven by the weight of a debt that he has assumed upon himself. The narrator is thrown into an involuntary acquisition of debts that entails repayment. The diverse characters in the novel are unified in their shared assumption on the subject of debts. This assumption is of a moral obligation that urges each of them to repay debts. Another common feature is the means employed to repay debts. Each of the characters is involved, to varying degrees, in subterfuge. Outright lying, judicious concealment or blasé ignorance of certain facts seem justified by the ends these acts seek to achieve.

I propose to undertake a reading of the nature of the debts, the reasons for their "existence" and the process of repayment, *i.e,* the role of debts as causal factors. The nature of the debt and specific creditor involved, provide sufficient clues to the character of the debtor. The paper is divided into two sections.

The first deals with the nature of debts and repayments within the lives of characters. The second part uncovers the modes of subterfuge deployed by characters in the process of debt acquisition and repayment.

I

The unnamed narrator's grandmother, Dadi, firmly believes that dues and debts *have* to be repaid. Her vocabulary bristles with references to ledgers, dues and debts (This register of accountancy/economics is noticed elsewhere in the novel as we shall see later). The fact that she has no unpaid debts pleases Dadi immensely, for "it gave her [Dadi] huge satisfaction that her family was solidly in the black" (2). Dadi rejoices in her participation in the freedom struggle because she believes that this act has made her children and grandchildren; "shareholders in the nation."

However, even the service that she renders to the nation and which earns Dadi the right to her place of pride in India, is suspect. Her participation in the Salt Satyagraha, her "public" phase is followed by a period of family life. The duties of being a wife and mother are in danger of distracting Dadi from working for India's freedom. She, therefore, founds a school for fallen women and takes to spinning. Both of these activities are commendable services towards the cause of liberation of the nation. However, it is Dadi's reluctance to join the Quit India Movement that reveals these services in their true form-namely conscience gratifiers. Similarly, Dadi's guilt (another demon) at her happiness when her husband is made a Companion of the Indian Empire, or C.I.E. (219) is assuaged only when she has "exorcised" her husband's wardrobe. His clothes, made of linen and twill, are replaced with homespun equivalents. Not content with this, Dadi decides that everything in the house, "was to be dressed in Khadi—this homespun armour of the nation—in—the—making" (220). This hectic activity is itself an indication of the need felt by Dadi to alleviate the guilt for being in the enemy camp by virtue of her British decorated husband. Thus Dadi chooses the passive mode in serving her nation (for staying away from the Quit India Movement). The methods she employs to pay her dues to the nation are merely token restitution of the debt invoked by Dadi's non-participation in the movement. Both her family and public roles are firmly circumscribed within the idea of debts.

Parwana expresses a desire to work in the kitchen of Dadi's house. Dadi's reaction to this request is an indication of true desires/beliefs warring with her urge to neutralise a debt. When Parwana offers to cook—"She [Parwana] begged to be allowed to make chapatis" (218)—Dadi is in a quandary. She cannot allow someone of uncertain origins to cook their food. The urge/compulsion to treat all humans beings as equal, the Gandhian ideal/injunction, is strong and cannot be ignored because of Dadi's own conviction. Dadi manages to satisfy both her predilections to treat all people as equal (and what better manner to prove this than accept food from someone of uncertain origins) and yet remain true to the dictates of her religion. Dadi has thus paid her debts to both nation and religion. Dadi justifies Parwana's role in cooking in a dazzling display of (feminine?) logic: Parwana used ghee in her cooking and hence, "made the cooking arrangement acceptably orthodox because it allowed Dadi to think of Parwana's chapatis as fried and fried food was acceptable, even from strangers" (219).

Dadi's commendable scruples in paying debts extends into her unwillingness to take anything that she has not earned. When her service to the nation is recognized and honoured, Dadi is distraught. The honour is a copper citation and a pension of four hundred rupees a month (3). Dadi's unwillingness to accept the honour stems from the fact that while she had actively participated in the Salt Satyagraha she was *not* involved in the Quit India Movement. When this movement began in 1942, "She (Dadi) looked away [...] (because) [...] she had grown used to paying her tithe to the Nation in the coin of social work" (4) and was unwilling to jeopardise family life. As Dadi admits to the narrator: "There had been guilt even then (1942), but her family, her home for fallen women and her spinning wheel had crowded it out" (5). But now, faced with the truth that she had shirked duty, Dadi quails from accepting the award of which she is "undeserving." She instructs her grandson to return the money and, "get a receipt for it" (4). As an added proof that

Dadi has taken nothing that she does not deserve she asks the officer in-charge to cancel her name off his ledger (3).

However, Dadi is forced to continue accepting the monthly pension cheques. Her grandson convinces her of his need for the money. As he puts it: "so in the end, for my sake, Dadi kept her stipend on" (5). Again we notice how Dadi embarks on a course of action that is repulsive to herself. However, Dadi manages to convince herself of the need for money, "always in the hope of eventually returning every paisa" (5). This course of action (retaining the pension for her grandson's sake) is repugnant to Dadi. However, the distaste is partially elided because of the conviction that this is a loan (which will therefore be repaid) for the sake of a loved grandson.

There is heavy irony in Dadi's debt of love. The payment of the final instalment of the loan on the grandson's zoom lens is made, and he now owns the lens. This payment which facilitates a permanent acquisition comes from Dadi's last drawn pension cheque. Her debt over, his "possession" completed, Dadi dies. The narrator says: "Dadi's last pension cheque had closed that chapter neatly" (7). Dadi's feeling of inadequacy, her nonparticipation in the Quit India Movement is symbolically erased in her last wish: her ashes be immersed in the Ganga at Benaras. This has nothing to do with the holiness of the river, rather "it was her salaam—in—death to the martyrs of 1942, many of whom came from Benaras and its neighbourhood, her last attempt to be part of the Quit India rebellion" (7).

This staunch belief in the debts that have to be paid percolates down to Dadi's grandson. Despite the selfishness that characterises the narrator's appeal to Dadi to retain her pension, it is his decision to repay the money ("when I paid her back as I swore I would," 5) that marks him as her grandson. The pedestrian casualness of this oath is belied in his ready acceptance and recognition of his debts to Dadi: "I volunteered to take the ashes—I owed her a debt and this was a good way of squaring the books" (7). Dadi's love becomes the demon haunting her grandson, again in the form of a debt (of love).

Thus, when the narrator finds that he is "knocking around in a time that didn't belong to me [the narrator]" (44), he fights the forces that hold him in his displaced position. However, with the failure of his plan to return to his own time/place he sets about creating a world for himself. This move of the narrator may be seen as a corelative to the immersion of Dadi's ashes in the Ganga and her unwillingness to accept the citation and pension.

Asharfi's words, "You're part of the family now" (48) are the first step in the narrator's insertion into the family order (and ordeal). Aware of the favour this has conferred on him, the narrator is scrupulous in doing his duty to the family, "partly because I owed them the truth for their goodness to me" (48). This preliminary and apparently innocuous step leads into deeper waters/debts. When Masroor is missing, Hassan's scheme to locate him [Masroor] inadverently includes the narrator. The narrator realises that he cannot refuse because "just yesterday Asharfi had claimed me for the family, every inch a Ganjoo. So it was natural for them to assume that I would be glad to help" (67). This enforced and obligatory participation in the affairs of Masroor's family binds the narrator to an extent such that he feels like, "a made—good migrant who had brought his family over" (207). The debt to the only family he has (now) triggers some actions. He follows Ammi and Asharfi on their trip to Simla and tries his best to ensure that Parwana and Asharfi do not meet. In return for this, the narrator does his best to persuade the family to stay on in India (instead of going to Pakistan) because, "I needed Masroor and his family too much to think objectively about the decision to stay" (376).

When the narrator is put up at the "akhara" by Chaubey he is obliged to Guruji for the sanctuary provided. This leads him (the narrator) to accept playing the role of Sita since he "was a refugee in the akhara and [...] I [the narrator] lived there at his [Guruji's] pleasure" (126). The narrator is therefore forced to drape himself in a saree and impersonate a woman!

Masroor is driven by the debts he had assumed upon himself. The nature of these debts can be described as "imaginary." Masroor reads his grandfather's *The History and Destiny of the Gangoos*. This hagiographic history is highly subjective and optimistic in tone. Its prophesies, almost assumes, a brilliant career for Masroor's father, Intezar. The realization that his father has cheated destiny by vanishing into thin air, convinces Masroor of his duty/debt. Intezar's absent presence is the demon to be exorcised by Masroor by vitiating the prophecies for his family. Therefore he (Masroor) must live up to the expectations written out. He fulfills this expectation (at least partly) by participating actively in the political events. Conscious of the slur his vanished father had made on the prophecy of an illustrious career, "Masroor had spent every waking minute of his life making sure that the same would never be said of him" (31). It is this certainty that leads Masroor to be a part of every political party or cause. He is a member of both the Congress and the Muslim league, at the historical moment when the two are in opposition to one another.

Ammi's debt is to the women whom she addresses through the Quarterly magazine, *Khatoon,* which she edits and publishes. Ammi realizes that she understands the needs of her readers. This realization demands that she reach out to them. This is the inspiration behind her magazine: "My khatoons, she [Ammi] would say, need to live, not learn" (16). Ammi believes that she knows what the women do not want—such as information about babies and housekeeping. By implication she makes herself aware of their real requirement. Ammi, therefore, deems herself to be the right person to provide these women with what they really deserve. For instance, her belief that first person narratives are more believable prompts Ammi to write all the articles herself, "so that the readers got exactly what she [Ammi] wanted [them to have]" (17). Curiously, the debtor [Ammi] becomes the real possessor of (intellectual, moral) property, the arbiter of her readers' choice. The reader, in turn, becomes indebted to her for her wisdom and advice. This marked reversal of roles is interesting.

II

Characters in the novel are dominated by the larger than life of Dadi (literally larger than life, since we meet her "alive" *after* her grandson has immersed her remains in the Ganga). The rules by which she lives—"No leftover food, no unpaid dues [...] she was determined not to become an object of charity" (1) descend into/onto her grandson. The other characters in the novel also exhibit an adherence to the rule of paying off debts. Nevertheless, it is Dadi's iron law, her slow death because of the guilt (at having accepted something that she does not deserve) that stand out in the tangled sequence of events in the novel.

It is suggested that Dadi's relaxation of her rule causes her death. In her life as wife, mother, freedom fighter and social worker, Dadi has several occasions when the need to pay debts presents a problem. As I have pointed out earlier, a few of Dadi's debts place her in the unenviable position of taking difficult decisions. When Dadaji is made a C.I.E., Dadi's guilt is alleviated by working towards the uplift of fallen women and devoting her time to spinning. However, one suspects that these laudable activities are motived by non-altruistic drives. Dadi revels in this social work. She feels this to be her duty to the nation and this leaves her with a free conscience to enjoy and share her husband's status as a C.I.E. Eating food cooked by Parwana is made acceptable by the ghee used, rather than be accussed of discrimination.

These situations are managed with ingenious subterfuge. Subterfuge is employed because Dadi needs to convince herself that her actions are above reproach. Once completed, Dadi ceases thinking of the reasons and methods of subterfuge. However, these old doubts and guilt resurface when she is honoured. At this point, the one act totally free of subterfuge—returning of the pension money—is sabotaged. Again Dadi is unwittingly dragged into pretending that the pension money will be paid back. On this occasion the guilt consumes Dadi before she can rationalize it sufficiently to bring life to a normal state.

The narrator taps the reservoirs of Dadi's love for him when she is persuaded to retain the pension. He (the narrator) convinces Dadi that she owes it to her grandson to help facilitate his career. The narrator is unable to repay Dadi for the pension cheques that he had misappropriated. However, he offers to pay his debt by immersing her ashes at Benaras, as she had desired. This straight forward acqueiscence with Dadi's wishes is nevertheless not quite *true* to her wishes. The ashes that the narrator immerses in the river belong to a different time frame (the 1990s). The Quit India Movement was in 1942 and Dadi did not join it. Here we cannot but observe how the narrator is almost forced into a situation that requires just the slightest prevarication of actual truth.

Similarly at the "akhara" the narrator is entrusted with some chores by Guruji. He takes on the responsibility of these in order to pay for this stay in the "akhara." This apparent appropriate repayment is not sufficient. Guruji asks the narrator to play the role of Sita in the Ramlila directed by him (Guruji). Again we notice how a *disguise* (as Sita), in other words, a subterfuge, is the only repayment that narrator can render in return for sanctuary at the "akhara."

For Masroor, subterfuge is something that he resorts to at the age of fourteen after he reads the history of the Ganjoos. He believes himself the only person capable of living upto the grand name of the Ganjoos. This belief induces in him the urge to do something. The struggle for India's Independence presents a glorious opportunity to prove himself and hence Masroor takes part in political activities: "There wasn't a cause or a party that he didn't make his own" (31). This spuriousness of purpose, the caprice evident in his joining both the Congress and the Muslim League, is no aberration, neither is his disappearance. The story of his disappearance cannot be accepted as the truth. The near-accident which convinces the narrator that Masroor is dead and the simultaneous appearance of his (Masroor's) figure on the side of the van are clever ploys to escape the situation brought on by his political views. Masroor appears disguised, as a clean shaven or a bearded man, at various points.

Ammi's mode of repaying debts appears realistic, perhaps because of its strange and bizarre nature. Ammi's subterfuge is perfect, so much so that we perceive it as the truth. This early acceptance of her subterfuge is also (perhaps) because of the end it seeks to achieve. While other characters are solely concerned with their debts, their position and hence *seek* subterfuge, Ammi is prompted only by her very real concern for women. This concern eliminates the danger of her actions being perceived as false. What is more, Ammi justifies her action because of her belief in the righteousness of these acts.

She has no need, therefore, to resort to lies and halftruths to justify her beliefs. Another illuminating feature is Ammi's self—sufficiency—she does not take any blame for untruths, no talk of praise for fulfilled promises.

The modes of repayment also vary. Jamal Mian offers verses from the Quran "scripted" as jalebis to stop the killing from coming to Lucknow (45). Bihari, the halwai who actually scripts these verses into jalebis, follows Jamal Mian's custom unquestioningly because it is a due that *he* (Bihari) has to pay towards keeping Lucknow peaceful. Haasan pays for his friendship with Intezar by becoming a part of the family. Haasan even erases his true identity, of being a Hindu, by using only the name of "Haasan." With this simple but effective change, he manages to be completely a part of Intezar's family.

These characters can be seen as representative of a time in India's history when the citizens were awakened to their duties. The stirring political situation affects personal relationships. Kesavan gives an indication of the national character of this awareness when he describes the refugees in the Old Fort. While some of these refugees repay their debts when they fall victim to diarrohoea and "return to the substance they had drawn from her" (361), others are unable to perform this simple duty because they are constipated. Still others, unsure of their creditors, develop stomach aches—which suggests that they neither pay their dues nor *avoid* payment.

On a larger scale these issues dissolve themselves into the larger question facing Indians then: do they opt for India or the newly formed Pakistan? It is this "overwhelming question" Kesavan finally poses: can the Indians accept sole credit of having paid their dues to their motherland by staying on? The narrator stays on because his foster family has paid the dues. They have earned for themselves, the right to stay on in India. This reading of the novel's conclusion is invited by Kesavan himself: Parwana, who has not earned her place in India by paying her dues, contemplates leaving India for England!

REFERENCE

1. *Kesavan*, Mukul, *Looking Through Glass*, New Delhi: Ravi Dayal, 1995.

11

"TRACING" VACUITIES: THE POETRY OF NIRANJAN MOHANTY

PROMOD K. NAYAR

Niranjan Mohanty is the poet of absences. In his poetry spaces are simultaneously vacuous and inhabited. Events, memories and people traverse the terrain which is otherwise barren and desiccated. This essay explores the absences, or more appropriately, the absent presences in Mohanty's poetry.

Mohanty has published three collections: *Silencing the Words* (1977), *Oh, This Bloody Game*! (1988) and *Prayers to Lord Jagannatha* (1994). His long poem "Krishna" is now being serialised in *Femina*, after its 1995 appearance in *Journal of South Asian Literature*.[1] In this essay I have used the three volumes and "Krishna" for purposes of analysis.

I

The theme of absent presences which forms all of Mohanty's poetry makes its first appearance in *Silencing the Words*. Absence here is either a going away after being present, or longing. The longing, in a sense, fills the absence with the "persona" of those absent and longed for.

There may be an absence of meaning where "words melt on beds/behind black curtains and never echo" ("Silencing the Words"). Meaning is lost in the dust which "echoes the silence/ and meanings of words in silence." This concern with a desiccation of meaning from words occurs in many other poems: "Wilderness" where "words melt in fugitive silence" and words are "obsolete," "The Search" wherein Mohanty suggests that "words swindle under the tangle weeds" and "Death of a Flower" in which a helplessness in signifying is presented ("Next morning/neither you nor I can mean/many things in words"). In most of these poems Mohanty first bestows a great deal of meaning upon words. The words may be part of songs, histories, a love tale or plain meditation. Mohanty then purges the same words of meaning, by suggesting the silence which envelops the very process of signification (as the lines from "Silencing the Words" and "Wildesness" quoted above suggest). A scar or trace of the *once perceived* meaning remains in the language/words. Thus, the absent presence is the trace of meaning in the melted, lost, tangled words. Mohanty subtly links these traces of meaning to people, thus suggesting that meaning in words is associated irretrievably with those who uttered them. Thus, all of Mohanty's protagonist speakers are intensely aware of past meaning (memory) and present vacuum. The absent presence of meaning thus becomes the trace of people themselves. This theme will recur with greater emphasis in Mohanty's later poetry, as we shall see.

I believe that it is precisely *in* such an evacuation of meaning that Mohanty's speakers live. The paradox suggested by Mohanty is this: the emptying of meaning makes the protagonist more conscious and therefore more alive. None of the speakers lose their minds or "die" in the poems, for that would suggest closure of signification. The mind which notes the evacuation of sense survives on traces, is more alert and alive now.

Longing is a method of vivification of the protagonist. It fills up the emptiness with the object longed for. It gives life to the non-available, the not here. Promises, like longing, ensures invoking of the absent. A promise calls up the not-yet-here to the moment. The promise as performative is hence like longing because it "produces" the unavailable. In *Silencing the Words* Mohanty suggests both longing and promise. There is apostrophe and prosopopoeia all of which give face/physiognomy, an identity to the absent. Fantasy, mythifying, memorialisation, promise even resurrection are involved in this process.

The duality of promise and longing allows the absent—alive

paradox of the protagonist. As noted earlier the protagonist's memory, longing or promise creates a heightened awareness. Through this Mohanty achieves a unique self for his speakers, a self rooted in the not-here, the absent.[2]

II

Oh, This Bloody Game! marks a regression into childhood. In this volume the absences of the protagonist's adulthood are clearly (or obscurely, since traces are shadowy) traceable to his childhood. Childhood trauma is a persistent trace, in Mohanty's second volume of verse. It also reinforces Mohanty's concern with personal history. The first two poems, "My Ancestors" and "History" suggest the underlying theme of this volume. Mohanty returns to the memory of grandmother's "stories/of ghosts, devils and witches" ("History—I), "ancient fables," the cradle, and the learning of alphabets "once again" ("History—II"). The archaeology and history of Konark marks "The Sun Temple at Konark" and ancestors figure in "A Winter Evening." Mohanty seeks the abandon of childhood when he had "with springs ... cooed among the leaves" ("Truth"). In "Ceremony of Silence" and "Years" he addresses issues of birth and childhood. Old people occupy "Ghost," "The Old Man," "Composition," "Learning," "Coming to Terms with Myself." Thus, ageing and childhood are frequent motifs here.

Closer reading reveals the scars of childhood in Mohanty's poems. With age the scars bite deeper in their traces. In "Oh, This Bloody Game of life, How did you Play, Dad?" Mohanty's speaker is troubled by his early childhood. Mohanty writes: "The echo of your voice makes me tremble." The reference is to the echo of a voice supposedly of the *dead* father. The fear it once aroused in the child is still the violence haunting the adult. This is the trace, the absent presence. It causes the "truant pen [to] slip away from the table." This poem, I believe, is the cornerstone of Mohanty's ouevre. One notes the way it prefigures all other poems in its motif of absent presences. Its conclusion is significant. Mohanty's speaker prays to his dead father to grant him

a pair of hands and a shoulder
to bear the altar of *my death*; a roof to house
my fears, a temple to worship your *gods*,
a strength to feed the *dead*
and a need to mingle in the *common lot*.

(emphasis mine)

The speaker looks forward to his own death (itself another promise of the not—yet—here, thus a trace of the future). and is inspired by his father's death. He seeks to feed the dead ancestors. The "common lot" might be a euphemism for the graveyard where all are equally placed (in lots ?), and death is the only lot common to all. Here the revenant (one who returns) of the dead (father) haunts the living. The ghost is also the *memory* of the father and the trace of the father's life in the speaker. Thus, memory and ghostliness are traces of the most important absence in the speaker's life: the father.[3]

In "Coming to Terms with Myself" Mohanty's speaker is once more troubled by ghosts. This time his siblings who died of cholera haunt him. A terrifying vision occurs where his dead brother and sister throw paper boats into the rain. It recalls the rainy day when the two died. This vision induces a fit of remorse and loneliness.

Mohanty's protagonist is scarified by his memories. On each occasion some event out of the past surfaces as trace. In "A Night that Keeps Crawling Towards My Blood" the speaker (now thirty five years old) recalls his childhood. The playfulness of his games, the sorrow of his grandmother's death, the father's coat all occur as visions. This combines with his awareness of the country's deteriorating law and order situation. This violence is also, in many ways, reminiscent of past violences. Thus, the specter of the country's violent past is recalled, re-lived today. In his mind the two scars (of childhood and present day violence) fuse. The trace has now burst into the open, and the past merely highlights the futility of the present.

III

The meditative verse of Mohanty's third collection, *Prayers to Lord Jagannatha* is very different from his earlier volumes.

There is mystico-religious tone here. The theme of absent presences figures again, and in a fashion that looks forward to "Krishna."

There is once more, the motif of promise, the unreachable and anticipation. The speaker prays to the God in a complaining tone. He accepts that God would not visit him. Yet there is a promise of familiarity in this not-yet-here God. Mohanty writes: "Let's remain unreachable/though familiar to each other." Here the God is invoked as a familiar face/person. The absent God is made present by familiarising Him. The speaker therefore continually identifies the idol as the God he waits for. This is a reversed prosopopoeia, where a faceless God is given form in the stone. It is this unattainable nature of the God which in a sense induces the prayer. In the promise/prayer, God "becomes" present.

Once again, ghosts and memories haunt the speaker. The speaker recalls the killing of Indira Gandhi, and mourns the violence. The strategy is the same: the death of the person, the absence, and finally mourning which brings back the dead, or rather keeps the dead alive in the present. It is now the whole country which mourns her death, thus reviving her. The speaker associates his memory of this major national event by recalling the death of his brother. The two mournings coalesce, and are typographically, narratologically placed *together* in the volume. The speaker has thus mourned for both together, at least by association.

The result is: one always recalls the other, the absence of one is also the absence of the other. Thus, both Indira Gandhi and his brother stay alive in their perpetual mourning. The country bears the trace of her killing, her absence and the speaker's brother is the absent present in his (the speaker's) life.

In a later section, Mohanty sketches his motif of absent presence. The speaker prays:

> Remind me always of the moments
> Of my births, of my previous deaths,
> Of my ecstasies and wounds.
> ....

So that I don't get frightened
At the intricate, intriguing
movements of *this* living.

(emphasis mine)

Here the speaker's present must be seen as reliving a previous birth. The "reminding" is a reliving. The previous experience shapes his present life. His past births mould his present. Mohanty thus invokes the Hindu idea of reincarnation, when his speaker returns, and is returned, to his previous births in this life. Much later (at the end of section v), the speaker prays: "Grant me/this much, I shall choose to die many times." The speaker is thus projecting, coalescing, telescoping the past, present and future. Both past and future become existent, present realities in his *current* life. *Prayers to Lord Jagannatha* is filled with images of faith, and eternal devotion. This is also a reworking of the absent presence theme. The speaker places faith in a tomorrow (like the promises), though he mourns the yesterday (like memorials). In section ix, for instance, Mohanty repeatedly uses the future tense to describe devotion ("would" occurs six times as a future tense in the space of fifteen lines). This is a section full of promises: of "undying devotion," faith and love for God. This faith and promise of future devotion prefaces the query "When will you come down to me/Oh Lord [...]?" I suggest that this faith invests the present with the God's presence, if at least as a promised arrival. The faith and promise in Mohanty are heralds, and therefore suggest imminent (future) presence even today. For it is in this faith of the speaker that the God lives today. Mohanty once more manages to concretise in today the "abstractness" of tomorrow's God. The beauty of Mohanty's poetry in this volume lies in the ease with which these apparently incongruous situations are brought together in the motif of absent presences.

IV

"Krishna," though not a collection, is worthy of assessment individually. A rare poem in its portrayal of the Radha Krishna story told from Krishna's point of view, "Krishna" is undoubtedly Mohanty's finest achievement yet.

"Krishna" is ideal for a psychoanalytic reading, though this is not my intention here. "Krishna" is about a series of absences of the beloved, her beauty and companionship.

Krishna's situation is a classic identity problem. Krishna identifies himself with the beloved, and simultaneously finds himself separated from her. Radha is for Krishna, his own self. Krishna on numerous occasions refers to Radha as a Mother figure to whom He goes "running." She is apostrophised as the source of Krishna's power, a temple, boat, hearts, home, sky and beginning. Krishna says: "Wherever I go, you guide me/like my mother." Radha is almost completely immanent. She occupies Krishna's flute, song, and sensation. The situation is a truly psychological association with the Mother figure. What follows is more interesting.

Radha goes away, and a "space/that separates your darkness from mine" exists between them. The absence of this figure *in* whom Krishna has known Himself, produces trauma. The separation denies any identity to Krishna. Thus the infant/ Krishna is troubled by the unreality of His existence:

> Can you tell me what is real?
> When you are away, the only thing
> Real is the distance [...]

When the mother/identifiable figure goes away, the absence makes the infant/Krishna suspect His own continuity. Krishna solves this situation in a manner characteristic of most of Mohanty's motifs. The beloved's immanence, being—in—Krishna is invoked as an absent presence. A certain quasi-ontological delusion is created. Radha is both within and without. Krishna's love is to be seen as a love of the absent presence within Him. There is, throughout the poem, a narcissistic state of Krishna. Note Mohanty's portrayal: on the one hand Krishna claims Radha as a mother figure, an external "love object proper" (to use Freud's phrase). He sees Himself as part of her and vice versa. At the same time Krishna is conscious of their mutual separation. He agonises over this. This image Mohanty uses to depict Krishna's dual, narcissistic and "outward-projected" love is purely Lacanian:

I am the mirror and the reflection
On it [...]

With the absence of the mirror, the child comes to terms with his identity by first perceiving himself in the mirror (Lacan). The "specular/speculative" gaze is turned onto *oneself* and away from the absent Mother figure. Here Radha the love object and Krishna's identity merge and separate. The absence of Radha sharpens Krishna's awareness of Himself and of Radha. Krishna, says, in Mohanty's memorable phrasing, "I glitter in her bangles," thus, stating His total identification with Radha. Yet Krishna also says:

Only when I listen to the sound
Of your footsteps [...]
I come closer of myself. I become
Myself once again.

Radha lives (on) in her absence, and in Krishna. Krishna loves the Radha in him and the Radha who comes from outside. Are the two distinguishable? The answer is difficult. Perhaps the absent presence of Radha is what *constitutes* Krishna as both subject and object. Mohanty's tale of this love retains the human element of a divine love story.

Niranjan Mohanty has thus revealed a persistent concern with absences. In his poetry the traces of such absences define, inform and invest all present being. Mohanty's poetry is superbly evocative for this motif (inspite of an unfortunate tendency to lapse into prolixity. Surely "concatenate," "gregarious," "catastrophic" are avoidable in his otherwise simple, mellifluous diction. Absent presences are more than oxymoronic. They form the potential for all existence. Set apart from other trite, self-conscious and bombastic verse of most Indian English poets today, Mohanty's sterling work is surely praiseworthy. Niranjan Mohanty's four sets of verse exhibit the finesse to handle extremely difficult motifs, such as the ones discussed above. One readily acknowledges the very present presence (inspite of his theme of absent presences) of a master poet in Niranjan Mohanty.

REFERENCES

1. *Mohanty,* Niranjan, *Silencing the Words,* Calcutta: United Writers, 1977; *Oh, This Bloody Game!*, Berhampur: Poetry, 1988; *Prayers to Lord Jagannatha,* New Delhi: Indus—Harper Collins, 1994; "Krishna", *Journal of South Asian Literature,* Vol. XXX, Nos. 1 and 2, 1995.
2. It is possible to see this particular feature of Mohanty's poetry as Romantic since the self is here characterised first and foremost by consciousness. All other objects exist only (as) in this self's promise/ memory/longing. Reading Mohanty as a Romantic poet might provide interesting results, though it is beyond the scope of this piece.
3. The fact that the father "lives on" in his son adds complexity to Mohanty's motif. In many ways, the father's ghost is carried within the son. This "returned" ghost is sometimes visible in the son's facial similarities with the father, as hieroglyphs (traces?) of the father's presence *inside.*

12

The Changing Trends in Indian Writing in English with Special Reference to Shobha De

JAIDIPSINH DODIYA

Raja Rao, R.K. Narayan and Mulk Raj Anand tried their best to give new identity to Indian Writing in English. Actually speaking it is gratifying that the 'Big Three' have lost none of their authenticity and appeal in the eighties, although their distinctive earlier works appeared in the thirties. Moreover, a new group of writers have arrived on the Indian scenario, for example—Anita Desai, Chaman Nahal, Kamala Markandaya, Arun Joshi, Dina Mehta, Salman Rushdie, Shobha De and the Booker prize-winner Arundhati Roy.

K.R. Srinivasa Iyengar rightly remarks: "When an Indian writer of fiction uses a learnt second language like English, he is actually recording a kind of half-conscious translation (from mother tongue into English) that has taken place in the mind. Most of our writers are bi-lingual, some equally proficient in English and the mother tongue, and some more in one than in the other. The background and the situations are usually Indian, but the characters may often be drawn from bilingual milieus. The need for expressing the values, verities and heart-beats of one culture in the language of another poses its own problems, and there is doubtless the inner urge to render in English the rhythms, idiosyncrasies, images, idioms and proverbs of the local speech. It is walking on a razor's edge for the Indo-Anglican Writer, for it is easier to slip into the ludicrous than to achieve satisfying results of transplantation and triumphant verbal communication."[1] Thus, one of the most outstanding characteristics of Indian Writing in English is that the background is Indian and the language though foreign, has adapted itself to the needs of the Indians. Now Indian English as well as Indian Writing in English has got its own identity.

Indian Fiction in English emerged out of almost six decades of intellectual and literary gestation that had begun in 1930s with the triumvirate of R.K. Narayan, Mulkraj Anand and Raja Rao as mentioned earlier. They were followed by a new crop of writers in the 1980s who dealt with a variety of subject in a casual and racy manner.

Actually speaking the most interesting aspect of the fiction at the turn of the present century from the Indian point of view is the emergence of new talent. A number of recent Indian novelists have produced significant novels, making a mark in the literary world. The most sensational literary event in the recent past was, probably, the publication of Salman Rushdie's masterpiece *Midnight's Children* which became an international success instantly in its release. It created a generation of young Indian novelists who eagerly followed his footsteps. Among these novelists, the notable ones are: Vikram Seth, Amitav Ghosh, Upmanyu Chatterjee, Shashi Tharoor, Mukul Kesavan and Rohinton Mistry.

These new novelists are aptly called by The New York Times "Rushdie's Children." In fact, these novelists have made very conscious efforts to include in their compositions the myths, humour and themes of the sub-continent. In short, Rushdie has been a trend-setter for the major Indian novelists writing in English. He told an interviewer in 1982: "I think we are in a position to conquer English Literature." Rushdie and his followers have tried their hand at writing novels on Indian themes.

In addition to Rushdie's "Magical realism" we find in Indian English novel a parallel tradition. The two strands of Indian Fiction are: that of "compassionate realism" exemplified by R.K. Narayan and more recently, Rohinton Mistry and that of "Pinwheeling intention" found in the writings of Rushdie, Shashi Tharoor and Allan Sealy. The former kind finds its culmination in Vikram Seth's *A Suitable Boy* (1992). This novel comes out with a Jane Austen like main plot. It tries to recreate the multitudinous life of post-Independent India on a scale unequalled by anyone before.

However, on reading Shobha De's novels, one can get some idea about the changing trends in Indian writing in English. Shobha De is one of the most eminent Indian novelists of our times. It is beyond doubt that she is one of India's best selling authors. She was born in Maharashtra in 1948 and was educated in Delhi and Bombay. She graduated from St. Xavier's College, Bombay with a Degree in Psychology. She began her career in Journalism in 1970 in the course of which she founded and edited three popular magazines—*Stardust, Society* and *Celebrity* and was consulting Editor to *Sunday*. She earned both name and fame while working as a free-lance writer and columnist for several newspapers and magazines.

In 1988, she wrote her first novel—the best selling *Socialite Evenings* and in 1990 she published *Starry Nights*. In all she is the author of nine books. Her works include *Socialite Evenings, Strange Obsession, Sultry Day's, Snapshots, Second Thoughts, Surviving Man* and *Speedpost*.

Shobha De as a writer is candid beyond our imagination. She is gifted with extraordinary ability to discuss every sensitive aspect in her fiction. She writes very frankly about each and every aspect of human-relationship. The orthodox people in India criticise her for her open discussion on sexual matters. But her fiction has got tremendous responses in several European Countries. Her fiction is read and enjoyed everywhere. As a writer she differs considerably from other Indian Women novelists writing in English. She believes in open-heartedness and very frank narration. She is the last woman to care for what others say about her. She is getting popular day by day. All classes of people read her novels. People appreciate the frankness of her style and the subject matter of her novels point to the gradual breakdown of human relationship. It is Shobha De who has broken away from-traditions. Her style has a vivacity which is reflected in novel after novel.

Shobha De is familiar with the life-styles of the so-called

elite societies of the metropolitan cities of India. Her keen observation and deep insight into human-relationships has enabled her to handle man-woman relationships deftly. In *Speedpost*, wherein she writes letters to her six children, Shobha De comes out as a compassionate, wise, witty and loving mother. *Speedpost* shares a mother's anxiety for her children. In her autobiography *Selective Memory: Stories from my life* Shobha De writes with impeccable skill and it is difficult to leave the autobiography midway. In *Starry Nights* Shobha De exposes the sham and hypocrisy of the Bombay film world. The competitive, commercial city of Bomaby has no time for failures. In such an undisguisedly materialistic environment, hedonism rules and there is no support system for the poor people. Shobha De can size up Bollywood because she was never a part of it and never wanted to be. Few can devastate hypocrisy the way Shobha De can.

Thus, Shobha De's fiction gives us a glimpse of the changing trends in Indian writing in English. Her modern and bold approach to literary creation has made her famous the world over. She has an observant eye and her narrative style is powerful and informative. On the whole she is a popular Indian writer who is considered to be a trendsetter.

REFERENCE

1. Iyengar, K.R. Srinivas, *Indian Writing in English.* 1962: rpt. Bombay: Asia Publishing House, 1996.

13

Imitiaz Dharkar—Voicing Protest

ASHOK K. TIWARI

Imitiaz Dharkar, born in Pakistan and brought up in England, is known to be a rebel against the narrow, orthodox manner in which Islam is interpreted and followed. She married Anil Dharkar, editor of the magazine *Debonair* and non-Muslim, violating a tenet of Islam and revealed herself to be a person with very independent and unconventional ideas.

Her discreet rebellion, especially with regard to the position and treatment of women in Muslim society, is evident in the *Purdah* poems which were published in 1989.[1] According to the exponents of Islam, the home is the proper domain of the woman. While it is the responsibility of the man to earn living, it is the woman's responsibility to make various household arrangements for the family. Another essential feature of Muslim culture is the segregation of women from the men-folk by the custom 'parde me bithana,' which means confinement of young women within the 'jenan khana' or women's quarters. The girls and women could go about only in a 'burka' or 'chaddar' or in a covered vehicle. There were restrictions on who they could talk to and the manner in which they had to speak. The seclusion was intended to protect their innocence and honour, there being a firm insistence on fidelity in this society.

However, the 'purdah' also developed into an instrument of masculine effort to keep low the spirit of independence in women and indirectly, to keep up the superiority of men.

Describing the condition of the orthodox patriarchal society in Islamic culture, Shibani Ray[2] says:

"In the male dominated Muslim Society Purdah is a male-imposed symbol of domination and seclusion symbolising the eclipse of Muslim Women's identity and individuality. The woman by wearing it subcribes to male domination and gives up her claim to personal liberty."

Some change in the situation may be observed in certain urban areas consequent to education, compulsion to seek employment, urge within the women to seek freedom and the desire to develop and express their individuality.

Shibani Roy's view of the effect of Purdah on Muslim Women is:

"Purdah affects a large area of a woman's life and precludes her from many areas of participation. This vitiates her life and produces a limited perspective and has a dementing influence on her entire personality. These oppressed characters feel protected and safe behind the purdah and consider that they are fortunate to have the means to secure themselves from the vicious world. Thus, a large part of the world remains a mystery to them."

In Purdah the focus is on a significant turning point in the life of a girl in Muslim society. At the threshold of youth, she attracts the attention of people around. Muslim society being conservative, it is important for a girl to preserve her modesty and honour so she must be taught decorum, shyness and caution The purdah is a device to protect the purity of a girl, checking the arousing of desire in the minds of men who see the young woman.

However, the purdah has a negative effect. It denies the girl the opportunity to seek learning and enlightenment, leading to the deadening of the intellect. It covers the intellect just as earth covers the dead person—cutting him off from the world of experience. The poet says:

"Purdah is a kind of safety.
The body finds a place to hide.
The cloth fans out against the skin
Much like the earth that falls
On coffins after they put the dead man in"

Another aspect of Muslim society that Imitiaz Dharkar criticizes is that women are not allowed to go into a mosque. There is fear that the women folk may, by some lapse of conduct, disgrace the men. Good men find it difficult to concentrate on prayer in the presence of women. Also, women may defile the mosque, as menstruation makes them impure.

It is ironical that the same blood nourishes the foetus and produces man. This thought offers the woman in the poem "Grace" some solace.

"Allah u Akbar"
You say the words to reassure yourself.
Your mouth clears.
God the Compassionate, the Merciful,
Created man from clots of blood.

There are other aspects of Imitiaz Dharkar's poetry and personality in the collection of poems "Postcards from God."[3] The poems are an expression of God's dissatisfaction with the state of the world—specially the milieu in which Imitiaz Dharkar lives. In the poem "After Creation," God seems to have hoped that there would be order in the world created by Him but seems to regret that in actuality there is a lot of disharmony in the world:

"When I began
it was a simpler world
Things perhaps, got out of hand"

The picture that emerges in the poem is that God is unhappy with the state of affairs in the world He created. There is a lot in the urban world of which Imitiaz Dharkar is a resident that troubles her, and the poet suggests, God.

In the poem 'Namesake," the poet expresses concern and compassion for a slum-dwelling child whose name is Adam. This child, living in Dharavi "survives" with pigs that root

Outside the door,
gets up at four
follows his mother to the hotel
where he helps her cut

the meat and vegetables, washes
it well, watches
the cooking pot over the stove
and waits, his eye-lids drooping
while behind the wall she sells herself
as often as she can before
they have to hurry home.

The world portrayed is one where a child has to labour for survival, and there is no joy in his life. This is a world of child labour, poverty and prostitution.

Imitiaz Dharkar reveals an interest in national politics but considers politicians responsible for much of the misery inflicted on common people. Her stance is clearly satirical. In "Seats of Power," Imitiaz satirizes the pre-Babri Masjid demolition inaction of the ruling politicians that results in communal violence. They seem to abet the holocaust. In the following lines the picture hinted at could be that of Prime Minister Narasimha Rao:

"The old man sits immobile,
only raises an eyebrow,
now and then, to flick
a lizard eye around the room

Speeches are read
A few points made
Somewhere in the city
a blade finds flesh

Here in this quiet evil room
permission has been given
for the carnage to begin."

In the poem "6th December 1992"—the day the Babri Masjid was demolished, the poet writes of the cunning, hypocritical politicians who fail to prevent communal violence—

"Glass leaders laugh
and the whole world can see
right through their faces
with their black tongues

And through the crystal night
the bodies begin to burn."

The poem "8th January 1993" paints a horrifying picture of the communal violence following the demolition of the Babri Masjid. There is arson, death, destruction and fear all around;

"The bolt bangs in
A match is struck and thrown
The burning has begun."

This poem carries the image of a cupboard left open in the looting—symbolizing the mouth of a person opening to scream, which is interrupted by death.

"a blistered cupboard
like a looted face
that opened its mouth
in a scream
that never found an end."

The poet is pained that ideals and values are not sought genuinely. They are lost in the hypocrisy of the politicians and religious leaders:

"The things we want are cliches
peace and brotherhood,
sanity, the goodness in ourselves.
What kind of words are these
to play with in this age
of fire and blood."

While in the Purdah Poems Imitiaz Dharkar comes across, as a feminist protesting with a lot of irony about the unsatisfactory situation of women in Muslim society, in the collection, "Postcards from God" she presents the response of a woman writer with feminine sensibility and sensitivity to a world where a lot has gone wrong with society and politicians have produced a situation of disorder, disharmony and violence, that God could not have planned for the world when He created it. She has the courage to criticize and protest.

REFERENCES

1. Tiwari, A.K., "Discreet Rebellion—The Poetry of Imitiaz Dharkar" in *Women's Writing* ed. Jasbir Jain, Jaipur: Rawat Publications, 1996.
2. Roy Shivani, *The Status of Muslim Women in N. India.* New Delhi : B.R. Publishing Corporation, 1979.
3. Dharkar, Imitiaz, *Postcards from God.* Penguin Books India Pvt. Ltd., 1994.

14

A Comparative Analysis of Arundhati Roy's *The God of Small Things* and Manju Kapoor's *Difficult Daughters*

JOYA CHAKRAVARTY

Stories have always occupied a special place in our lives. Stories recorded in Epics and Scriptures or transmitted orally, instruct us in the art of handling the dilemmas of existence and equip us to face life's problems.

Both Arundhati Roy's novel *The God of Small Things* (GOST)[1] and Manju Kapoor's *Difficult Daughters* (*DD*)[2] jointly weave a tale which instructs and transmits to the readers, the authors' knowledge of the Indian mind-set.

The Narrative genre is a way of thinking and reasoning and a writer uses the narrative technique to express his own thoughts as well as the thoughts of the characters.

A writer endeavours to express the diverse cultural experiences of the people. In Post-Colonial Literatures people are bound by their reminiscences of the past, and by the sacrifices made by the glorious and great men. In the present they are bound by the common will to give a shape to and put into effect their future programmes. Gayatri Chakravarty Spivak observes in "Marginality in the Teaching Machine" [...] "post-coloniality is a mode of existence whose importance and fragility would be destroyed by techniques of specialist knowledge as they work with strategies of power"[3] (74). Critic Homi Bhabha observes, "The post-colonial perspective [...] forces a recognition of the more complex cultural and political boundaries that exist on the cusp of these often opposed political spheres"[4] (173).

Indian culture is a composite heritage and its multidimensional character helps to bind the people. British colonialism and the education that the British imparted, brought about an awareness in the minds of the people. The Indians initially imitated their masters. However, after some time cracks began to appear in this relationship and the colonizers had to face protests from the colonised people. Gandhi succeeded in arousing national consciousness and people began to value their culture and Indianness. Thus, emerged the concept of a national identity. People longed for their mother culture, they longed for the pre-colonial state. The need of the hour was to maintain one's identity rather than submit to the British hegemony. Inter-regional interaction began and this helped to shape the concept of a national identity.

Independence brought with it displacement (partition of India) and disillusionment. The post-colonial writers had to re-interpret and re-write various issues from a post-colonial perspective. Colonialism had given security—one inhabited a fixed world. Post-colonial world was a new world—not firm, the ground seemed to be moving. The continued imposition of alien political, economic and social philosophies could not do away with the problems of young India.

The writers writing in the post-independence era began to use language in a very effective way. Writing from the perspective of the fragmented, marginalised, racially discriminated people, the Indian writers from the 1960s onwards began to question the imposition of social practices, which were arbitrary. The multi-culturalism of India highlighted the cultural differences of the people. New writers began experimenting with the form and literary works associated with post-colonial experiences of migration, identity crisis, diaspora began to be written.

In *The God of Small Things* and *Difficult Daughters* the writers portray pictures of the contemporary times by an effective use of language. Roy experiments with the form of the language to write a hackneyed story—a high caste woman falls in love with a man of the lower caste. The result is obvious—class discord, secret rendezvous, arrest and annihilation. The novel begins with death, is interwoven with memories mostly tragic and ends in a feeling of loneliness and despair—it is not a lived-happily-hereafter ending. Roy's resorting to the use of the language metaphor is essential to our understanding of Indian culture and Indian post-colonial scenario. *Difficult Daughters,* too, begins with death, is interwoven with memories and ends in a feeling of melancholy and depression. *Difficult Daughters is* partly travelogue, partly analytical and partly literary history. But this is essentially a story of three generations and is interspersed with historical facts. The regional culture of Amritsar and Lahore can be felt in some of the specific actions performed by the characters, the words are loaded with meaning in conformity with the prevalent values. *Difficult Daughters* discusses the life of Virmati in Amritsar and Lahore. Nowadays the journey from Amritsar to Lahore takes about 15 hours. What is significant is the fact that ever since the partition the land which separates the two cities is mined with history.

In *The God of Small Things Roy* reveals the agony of Estha and Rahel as they watch in fear the atrocities heaped by the police on Velutha—"History in live performance" (309).

In *Difficult Daughters* Virmati' fails in her attempt to commit suicide and she is punished for her behaviour by being locked in a godown. The dismal state of Virmati's mind cannot be fathomed by her people. Both the novels deal with the theme of hunger for love and the sense of alienation. The characters in the works of both these novelists suffer from humiliation and exploitation by the elders, parents and society. Both the novels highlight the breakdown of communication. In both the novels there is no solidarity and sympathy for the sufferer—the victim must continue to suffer alone and in silence.

Though the authors depict different time frames, their handling of social institutions and characters strikes a note of similarity. Be it Romeo-Juliet, Shirin-Farhad, Virmati and Professor, or Ammu and Velutha, societal behaviour is stereotyped. The reactions of society, which the writers mirror in their works, are reflective of the fact that over the years societal behaviour, as far as lovers are concerned, has not changed. In India human reaction to lovers generally begins on a note of disapproval. Society refuses to identify with the plight of the lovers. Both the novels highlight the state of women—a woman is a commodity to be used and misused—her feelings are never called into account. To possess her completely is the aim of man because he knows that only complete possession will bring complete control. Gayatri Chakravarty Spivak, while commenting on Mrinal Sen's film 'Genesis' notes "The men are obsessed by the question of paternity [...] a point is made that does not apply only to the 'third world' or 'marginals'; the point that the real issue in the overthrow of mother right is not merely ownership but control" (74). *The God of Small Things* shows both gender oppression and class oppression—Ammu and Velutha share and suffer oppression at the hands of society.

As stated earlier, the hunger for love and the theme of alienation dominates both the novels.[5] Virmati takes complete care of her siblings. But she desires love and affection from her mother, which is repeatedly denied to her. Her mother thrusts her away from her side and reminds her to wash the dishes or cook the evening meal. Surrounded by clamorous children and with love denied, Virmati begins to value her privacy and freedom. Her behaviour alienates her from her family. The twins Estha and Rahel, after being separated, feel alienated. Partition alienates people and highlights the political discord between nations and families. Lush green Kerala denies a woman a place of her own. There is a strong patriarchal bias against women in the division of property. The women are also at a disadvantage as far as space and freedom are concerned. Ammu and Chacko have been educated differently and when both return to Ayemenem, Chacko assumes his position at the head of the table while Ammu has no *locus standi*. Chacko tells Ammu "What is yours is mine, and what is mine is mine also."

Virmati is brought up in an Arya Samaj house and is sent to a Samaj school and college. Her education brings about an ideological change in her and transforms her. The Arya Samaj had encouraged women's education and discouraged child marriage. The Arya Samaj movement was basically Hindu in spirit. It tried to counteract conversion to Christianity. In *The God of Small Things* Roy delineates the lives of the Syrian Christians. Some of these were untouchables who had converted to Christianity. Having become Christians they neither got the advantage of governmental reservations nor societal acceptance. They thus have an indefinable attitude. In *Difficult Daughters,* Kasturi's praying before a picture of Christ prompts Kasturi's uncle to start an Arya Samaj school for girls. Kasturi could visualise no future for Virmati other than being a good wife and mother like herself. Thus, education was important from the matrimonial point of view only. Virmati pursues further education at Lahore not because she is career oriented, but because she wants to escape from the reproaches of her family. Virmati's cousin Shakuntala makes use of her education and chalks out plans for her own life.

Marriage is another issue in both the novels. Ammu's marriage breaks down and she is made to feel like a black sheep of the family. She had married out of caste and then had a divorce—this further weakens her stand. Chacko marries an English lady who walks out of the house after a few years. Chacko returns home and his sexual needs are conveniently fulfilled through his mother who bribes and procures young factory women for him. When his ex-English wife comes with her daughter Sophie Mol (by Chacko) she is given a warm welcome at Ayemenem. Ammu and her twin children Rahel and Estha feel humiliated by the treatment meted out to them by Mammachi, Baby Kochamma and Chacko. Ammu had never experienced love and security at home. Her father, a renowned etymologist, would often turn Mammachi and Ammu out of the house on chilly winter nights in Delhi. Ammu marries hoping thereby to get out of the clutches of a brutish father. But her husband's alcoholic bouts are too much for her to bear and she returns to Ayemenem to lead a bleak and lonely life. The physical and emotional vacuum in her life brings her in contact with Velutha—the god of small things. She crosses the river at night to meet her lover while Virmati in *Difficult Daughters* tries to drown herself in the canal at twilight. Both the river and the canal are important metaphors in the novels. Virmati knows that if she expresses her love openly for Professor Harish Chandra it would bring embarrassment to her and her family. She feels insecure and rootless and desires to go to Lahore to pursue higher studies. She must marry, for that alone will give her security and certainty. She becomes the Professor's second wife and this formal stamp to her relationship brings her back into the social fold. Ganga, the Professor's first wife, thinks marriage is a social and religious institution and is happy to take care of his needs. But Ganga is unable to understand the Professor's craving for an educated companion. Educated Virmati fills the mental and intellectual vacuum in the Professor's life. Virmati's daughter Ida is strong and clear-headed. She terminates her marriage when she is denied maternity by her husband. She breaks free of the nuptial ties. There is a strength and determination in her which is lacking in Virmati.

Ammu, however, is not fortunate enough to marry Velutha. The policemen swoop down on this innocent, unarmed "paravan" and the twins watch in horror "History in live performance" (309). After this incident Ammu is thrown out of the house. Ostracized from home and society, Ammu lives and dies alone in a dirty tenement in a far away place.

Manju Kapoor's novel enables us to study three generations of women—Kasturi, Virmati and Ida. These and the other female characters in the novel enable us to get an idea of the feminist struggle against biases. *Difficult Daughters* discusses the period during India's struggle for freedom. While reading the novel one gets the impression that a woman's life is like the life of a nation. Like an investigative journalist Ida struggles to reconstruct her mother's life. In *The God of Small Things* Roy reveals a facet of India which is at times difficult to accept. The Indian's habit of easing himself is portrayed in a putrid and revolting manner. It is difficult for the reader to identify with some of the things. *The God of Small Things* seems to be showcasing India on its window panes for all the world to sneer and titter. In Roy's writing there is a certain kind of self-derisiveness: as if she is making fun of the Indian way of life.

Post-colonial India continues to be poverty-stricken stratified and inegalitarian. Indian English writers, feeling alienated from the national culture, try to present a picture of India which still suffers from the colonial hangover. This image of India has found acceptance in the West. Great Britain probably could not get over the fact that she had lost control over India hence British publishing firms were eager and quick to publish novels wherein India was presented in an adverse light.

Post-colonial Indian society lives with its illusions and dreams. At times reality is harsh but need we present only this picture of India? In India, English language still continues to be the language of the elite, modern and educated people. We teachers of English Literature have been fed on a diet of deconstructionism, post-colonial theories and subaltern studies. Our dreams have been doctored and we sail unanchored in troubled seas. We seem to belong nowhere. But India still resides in villages like Ayemenem and it is our duty to uphold the Indian culture and consciousness which are fundamental to our way of life. Some of the most admirable and enduring qualities of Indian society have been viewed from a wrong angle, for instance, Indian resilience and forbearance which are born of a large and comprehensive view of the reality of the world—mutable and transient—are depicted as an inherent weakness in the Indian character.

Indians by nature have a tendency to take everything in their stride—they know that human actions are just like small ripples in an ocean and therefore, must not be taken too seriously. In fact not to take life too seriously is not a helpless surrender to an abstract metaphysical philosophy but a sign of wisdom which concerns itself with the inner core and not the outer surface.

Again, post-colonial hangovers are rather over-emphasized in these novels. But there is little indication of the possibilities of a strong resurgence of a new set of values in India as an independent nation. The average Indian is in quest of a post-colonial frame of mind—we are post-colonial only politically, our thinking is still colonised as we are perpetually suffering from an approval complex.

REFERENCES

1. Arundhati Roy, *The God of Small Things.* Delhi: India Ink, 1997. All quotations are from this edition and the page numbers are given besides them.
2. Manju Kapoor, *Difficult Daughters.* Delhi: Penguin, 1998. All quotations are from this edition and the page numbers are given besides them.
3. Gayatri Chakravarty Spivak, *Outside in the Teaching Machine.* London : Routledge, 1996. All quotations are from this edition and the page numbers are given besides them.
4. Homi Bhabha, *The Location of Culture.* London: Routledge, 1994. All quotations are from this edition and the page numbers are given besides them.
5. See Santosh Gupta ed. *Contemporary Indian Literature Positions and Expositions.* Jaipur: Rawat, 2000.

15

OF PLACES AND THINGS: THE POETRY OF KEKI N. DARUWALLA

RAVI NANDAN SINHA

Often called a landscape poet, Keki N. Daruwalla has written some of the most powerful and vivid poetry about places. It is, however, somewhat misleading to call a poet this or that only, primarily because such classification tends to highlight certain elements in a poet's work at the expense of other, possibly equally powerful, elements in his work. Secondly, such definitive classification militates against the essentially polysemous nature of good poetry. The term 'a landscape poet' does describe Daruwalla, but only partly. Landscape painting, if this extra-literary term can be used for poetry, is one of the many elements in the intricate pattern of his poetry. The poet seeks to transfer to the reader, a complete poetic experience. Even in the so called 'landscape poems' the focus may not essentially be on the landscape as much as on the poet's emotional, intellectual and even moral response to it.

Daruwalla considers himself a writer rooted in the rural landscape. R. Parthasarathy quotes him in *Ten Twentieth-Century Indian Poets*, "I am not an urban writer and my poems are rooted in the rural landscape. My poetry is earthy [...]."[1] The earthiness of his poetry exhibits itself in a description which, according to Gopal Gandhi, has "a three-dimensional quality"[2] about it. In his poem 'In My Father's House' Daruwalla describes a winter scene :

Nothing is new
around this place
except the snow,
except the quiet
monastic vows
of Wizened bark
on skeleton tree.
The ribs too are a monastery
when seasons do not change within.[3]

The loneliness is suggested by using words 'monastic' and 'monastery' both of which have been derived from mono, *i.e.*, single. The desolateness of the place has been suggested by words like 'Wizened bark,' 'skeleton tree' and 'the ribs' where seasons do not change. The stillness is accentuated by

the high—singing, groaning, whining
of the iron-sheet roofs.
with flailing arms
and weird voices,
the wind beats
on the house like surf. (*Crossing of Rivers*, 56)

All this prepares the reader for the idea of death, suggested by "rotting muscle," a poppy taking "root on a mole" and a tuber "wondering through the eyes" (*Crossing of Rivers*, 57). This poem is one of the many instances of the poet's ability to blend the landscape with emotion. After every aspect of the poem has been discussed, there remains a residue of meaning. Such poems underscore the validity of Irving Massey's remark, "The creation of an imaginary world which has substantial reality is a normal and legitimate activity of poetry but the reality of the world so created cannot rest in words, it must be an experienced phenomenon."[4] In the poems of Daruwalla the experiential component of reality is extremely prominent.

In his collection of poems entitled *Winter Poems*, there is a long poem (or, a sequence of poems) called 'Hunger—74.' In a matter-of-fact style the poet describes the failure of rains:

They sprained their necks looking up for clouds,
the light so harsh that corneas
started smoking at the edges.[5]

The disappearance of hope is gradual. First, "the clouds flashed past like migratory birds":

> Then in answer to some unheard utterance
> from the parched lips of this land
> they settled like birds come to roost.
>
> (*Winter Poems,* 25)

In the absence of rain everything looks ugly. The sun is "sharp and stinging," the moon "a bloated/well-fed must melon" and the stars "lighted ulcers on the sky's belly." The sky is made of "bone." The temperature sinks like "a cement sack." Then comes March

> March-hail, and the last glimpse of a lean orion
> as he tightens his belt
> around his emaciated waist.
>
> (*Winter Poems,* 26)

The April wind is "hyena-mouthed." This wind turns to hot summer winds

> Animal-tongues hang out. A woman ends her
> thirst in a dry well, one babe in each arm-pit.
>
> (*Winter Poem,* 26)

Keshav Malik, in his review of *Landscapes,* compares Daruwalla to "a war-correspondent on the battle scene giving out commentaries from moment to moment."[6] But here in this poem, as in many others, the detailed description is made live by the poet's sense of empathy. In this sense, Daruwalla is much more than a mere war-correspondent. Of course, his ability to describe a scene is exceptional, a quality which P.D. Chaturvedi terms "almost Hardyesque."[7] He goes on to say:

> He paints a landscape which acts not only as a backdrop to his poems, but also participates in its action and movement. The essential poetic significance of the landscape is the question of reflection which that scene evokes in us.[8]

'Crossing Chorhoti' in *Landscapes*[9] takes the reader past "the smell of mint behind us" beyond "the world of pollen and drifting spore" into a world of "saw-toothed crags/touched with mineral oxides":

The evening was beryl-blue
as we left the grass-bowl of Barahoti
and reached the wind shadow
in a place which has no grass, no trees,
no dust, you cannot see the wind.

(*Landscapes,* 31)

The journey is difficult where

Dreams came ghost-lit
And shortly guttered
like the butter lamps of Tibet.

(*Landscapes,* 32)

Throughout the poem the poet refers to strong chilly winds and to the Lamas, the Buddha and the "mother-goddess Dolma." The poem occasionally acquires the intensity of a prayer,

Goddess I am seeking shelter
from the approaching storm.
I seek the cavern-aspect
of your embracing form
which smothers in lap-darkness
yet lights the spinal reed
From your womb all proceed,
Into you all recede.

(*Landscapes,* 33)

The divine presence is evoked once again when the poet describes "fifty Indian peaks" with

snow and the spray-hangover
of icefalls and the blue of distance,
as if some god had with a palette-knife
honed the landscape with ethereal colours.

(*Landscapes,* 33)

The poem ends with the words of the Buddha haunting the poet:

I recalled the Buddha's words and deflected them :
'Opened wide are the gates of immortality,
ye that have eyes to see release your faith.'

But irony haunted me even at this height;
Kailash was veiled by a cloud layer of white.

(*Landscapes*, 34)

It is easy to see how finely are landscape and thought intertwined.

A very large number of poems of Keki N. Daruwalla may be called river poems. Mention may be made of 'Dawn,' 'Vignette I,' 'Vignette II,' 'Vignette III,' 'The Dip,' 'Mother' and many other similar poems in which the river is the subject. There is a great deal of variety in these 'river poems,' they mirror both the harsh and, as A.N. Dwivedi says in discussing 'The Parijat Tree' "the mild aspect of landscape."[10] The poems in his third book *Crossing of Rivers* make use of the river motif in many ways. Social, religious and cultural aspects of a river are brought to life in vivid and vibrant poetry. The central metaphor of the book is the Ganga which in the words of Vrinda Nabar "appears here with all its primal, religious, and emotive connotations. The river's rhythm is that of life and death, of birth and rebirth, of passion and rejection [...]."[11]

'Boat-Ride Along the Ganga', the first poem in *Crossing of Rivers*, reverses the perspective in the sense that here the land is seen from the river and not the other way round. The poet is part of the river riding upstream in a motor-boat at dusk:

Slowly the ghat-amphitheatre unfolds
like a diseased nocturnal flower in a dream
that opens its petals only at dusk
Palm-leaf parasols sprouting like freak-mushrooms
brood over platforms that are empty.

(*Cross of Rivers*, 11)

There is a sense of the unreal in the opening of the "ghat-amphitheatre" which unfolds like "a diseased nocturnal flower in a dream." The idea of disease is reiterated in the simile of "freak-mushrooms" used for parasols on the banks of the Ganga in Varanasi. Mushrooms can be poisonous, too especially if they are "freak" ones. The poet is not alone in the motor-boat

Outlines blur in the apoplectic gloom
as the *panda* points our Dasasvamedh.

I listen avidly to his legend-talk
striving to forget what I chanced to see:
the sewer-mouth trained like a cannon
on the river's flank.

(*Crossing of Rivers,* 11)

The contrast between the timeless "legend-talk" of the *panda* and the 'sewer-mouth" trained "like a cannon" symbolises the violence done by the city to the river which makes it holy.

The journey along the Ganga is punctuated by "the pyres" which make the poet bow his head to "the finality of fate." The "heat-haze rising from the fires" makes everything "shimmer, dance, levitate."

You face reality on a different plane—
Where death vibrates behind a veil of fire.

(*Crossing of River,* 11)

There is death but no lament; this "the mourners learn from the river." The focus in the poem, then, is on death. The river and Varanasi provide the context in which death is seen. But 'Boat-Ride Along the Ganga' is much more than a mere description of the burning ghats of Varanasi seen from a moter-boat. The *panda* who calculates

the amount of merit that accrues to you

(*Crossing of Rivers,* 11)

represents all that Varanasi stands for an average pilgrim. It is a place to die in and to achieve instant salvation. Is there hidden satire in these lines? A.N. Dwivedi takes up the question while discussing the 'Second Vignette':

> It is not that Daruwalla deliberately denigrates Varanasi : he rather discovers it to be no better than many other ancient cities of the Hindus. Despite the fact that it is taken to be the abode of gods and goddesses. His 'seeing' enables him to grasp things as they really *are,* not as they *ought* to be.[12]

While it is largely true that much of Daruwalla's poetry can be characterized as 'realistic' (though this characterization itself will be somewhat inadequate) one cannot run away from the feeling that there is a moral stance in his poetry. His work may not consciously be a social gesture yet his ethical preferences are often obvious.

REFERENCES

1. Daruwalla, Keki N. cited from Parthasarathi, R. ed. *Ten Twentieth-century Indian Poets,* New Delhi: OUP, 1979, 12.
2. Gandhi, Gopal, 'Bees of the Invisible' Review of *Landscapes, The Book Review,* Vol. 11, No. 4, Jul.-Aug. 1987, 17.
3. Daruwalla, Keki N., 'In My Father's House.' *Crossing of Rivers,* Delhi: OUP, 1976, 56 (All further references to this book are to this edition).
4. Massey, Irving, *The Uncreating Word.* Bloomington, 1970, 128.
5. Daruwalla, Keki N., 'Hunger -74.' *Winter Poems.* Delhi: Allied Publishers Private Ltd., 1980, 25. (All further references to this book are to this edition).
6. Malik, Keshav, Review of Landscapes *Indian Horizons,* Vol. 36, No. 3-4, 1987, 49.
7. Chaturvedi, P.D., 'New Poetry in India,' *Commonwealth Quarterly,* Vol. 4, No. 13, March 1980, 116.
8. *Ibid.,* 116.
9. Daruwalla Keki N., Crossing 'Chorhti', *Landscapes.* Delhi: OUP, 1987, 31.
10. Dwivedi, A.N., 'K.N. Daruwalla: The Painter of Rural Landscape,' Papers on Indian Writing In English (ed.) A.N. Dwivedi. Delhi: Amar Prakashan, 1991, 172.
11. Nabar, Vrinda, 'Keki N. Daruwalia. Poetry and a National Culture,' *Osmania Journal of English Studies,* XIII, No. 1, 1977, 10.
12. Dwivedi, A.N., 'K.N. Daruwalla: The Painter of Rural Landscape.' *op. cit.,* 176.

16

NARRATIVES OF EXCLUSION: TONI MORRISON'S "BELOVED" AND LAXMAN GAIKWAD'S "THE BRANDED"

NAFISA HATMI

Hierarchical distinctions of colour, class, caste, sex and religion are dominant tropes of oppression operative in a society and are responsible in perpetuating systems of inequality. This paper attempts to establish how the black women and Dalits as minorities have been categorically denied not only literacy but the most minimal possibilities of decent human life. They encounter deprivation which determines their limiting and limited circumstances. Their entry into the mainstream is made difficult not merely by prejudices and restrictions but also by psychological boundaries they internalize as they develop in a social structure that historically has excluded them. Toni Morrison's *Beloved* and Laxman Gaikwad's autobiographical novel *The Branded* are profound and shattering narratives of their exclusion through which they aim to affirm their self-hood which though their own has been "othered." They need to write and reclaim the story of their exclusion in order to define themselves.

The attempt to unite the voices of Dalit and the black, the Black Women in particular finds justification in the fact that due to their status as lowest of the low they have to face and accept that there is no escape from the harsh reality of their existence and so Claudia in *The Bluest Eyes* realizes "being a minority in both caste and class we moved about on anyway hem of life, struggling to consolidate our weaknesses and hang on or to creep singly up into the major folds of garment,"[1] as Sula in *Sula* discovers that she and her friend Nel are "neither white nor male means that all freedom and triumph was forbidden to them"[2] and still worst Sethe in *Beloved* is pained at being deprived of her very essence, her maternal milk. "There was no nursing milk to call my own. I know what it is to be without milk that belongs to you."[3] And in a similar way Laxman Gaikwad realises what it means to be "born in rejected ostracized community [...] denied an innate humanness by all and sundry forced to live a life no better than that of a godforsaken animal."[4]

The subject of slavery has a particular fascination for Toni Morrison as it enables her to explore the implications of representing slavery on the "real slaves" and their descendants who are no longer slaves. Her intention of writing slave narratives observes Marilyn Sanders "is not to convince white readers of the slaves humanity, but to address black readers by inviting us to return to the very part of the past that many have repressed, forgotten or ignored."[5] All her novels specially *Beloved* offers a painfully compelling, detailed account of slave humiliation and oppression so that the black life on American soil is recorded, examined and understood for its complexity and significance and not excluded in a new version of American history.

Beloved is set during the end of Civil War when violence against black reached its climax. Through flash backs Morrison takes us to more distant period when slavery was practised in the South. The narrative circles around a group of slaves who once lived on a plantation in Kentuci—"Sweet Home." Each slave has a drastic story to tell and each share a common burden of exploitation, ostracization and oppression and their stories gradually merge into a single story.

Sethe the central character of the novel is a runaway slave woman and slave mother who feels alienated and repressed under the burden of her past. Her past comes to us in bits and pieces in form of stories and flashbacks. Paul D., one of her companion at 'Sweet Home', comes after eighteen years and his presence makes Sethe speak. She recalls the incidents of her racist and sexist oppression. The worst she suffers is when the boys at the farm steal her breast milk, they milk her like a cow while her own children separated from her are deprived of their mothers milk. The tree like scar mark tells the horrible story of physical torture. The cruel school master encodes scars on her back when she complains about the boys who took away her milk. Sethe decides to leave 'Sweet Home' to escape torture. Her children leave before her but her husband Halle does not come at the appointed hour and is lost to her forever. Under such stressful conditions Sethe commits her desperate, violent and loving act of infanticide. We almost neglect the perversity behind her action and sympathize with her when she admits "why I did it. How if I had not killed her she would have died and that is something I could not bear to happen to her" (*Beloved*: 200) because we are made to realise observes Roberta Rubenstein that "when people are dehumanized by poverty, prejudice or restricted opportunity for growth of the self, the capacity for relationship may be radically perverted."[6] Sethe kills Beloved to protect her from slavery. The burden of guilt and past is heavy to bear and Sethe longs for her dear, dead baby Beloved the name she was allowed to engrave on the tombstone by exchanging sex.

Toni Morrison makes successful use of folklore by invoking the ghost of Beloved. It is through the ghotic presence of Beloved that Sethe relives her past. Beloved's presence allows Sethe to convey recollections, she could never utter to anyone else. Like Sethe her mother in law Baby Suggs has also suffered loss of her beloved ones "all of Baby's life as well as Sethe's own, men and women were moved around like checkers. Anybody Baby Suggs knew, let alone loved, who had not run off or been hanged, got rented out, loaned out, bought up, brought back, stored up, mortgaged, won, stolen or seized" (*Beloved*: 23). Baby had eight children, all left her and only Halle, Sethes husband brought her freedom when "it did not mean a thing" (*Beloved*: 23). However, unlike Sethe she did not resort to destruction. She tried to give meaning to her life by helping other runaway slaves. She became almost a preacher encouraging her people to live with dignity by calling them to love themselves—"in this her place, we flesh; flesh that weeps, laughs, flesh that dances on bare feet in grass.

Love it, love it hard [...]. More than lungs that have yet to draw free air. More than your life holding womb and your life-giving private parts, hear me, now, love your heart. For this is the prize (*Beloved*: 88). The narratives of Sethe and Baby Suggs raise questions like "Do slave women have no right to have a family? Should they be excluded from the experience of owning children?" The glaring reality that their economic destitution and psychic abjection undermines the bonds that attach family members together becomes evident.

Paul D., Sethe's friend from the Sweet Home plantation comes to Sethe's house in the countryside near Cincinati after eighteen years. Paul D. like Sethe is haunted by the memories of slavery. He has witnessed the physical and psychological destruction of his fellow Sweet Home men Paul A. being caught and hanged. Sixo being caught and burnt alive. He too has suffered physical torture after having been caught while running away. He was sold in chain with a bit in his mouth. Like Sethe he refuses to speak about his suffering. His memories have been locked, "one by one in his chest. By the time he got to 124 nothing in this world could pry it open" (*Beloved*: 113). It is the ghost of Beloved that helps in restoring Paul D. to himself. The scene of Paul D.'s intercourse with Beloved is suggestive of his bodily cure and liberation:

> She moved closer with a footfall he did not hear and he did not hear the whisper that the flakes of rust made either as they fell away from the seams of his tobacco tin. So when the lid gave he did not know it. What he knew was that when he reached the inside part he was saying, "Red heart. Red heart" (*Beloved*: 117).

Paul D. is not totally broken by slavery. He struggles to create meaningful existence and therefore expresses a desire to Sethe that they could make life together and thus, "He wants to put his story next to her" (*Beloved*: 273).

Sethe, Baby Suggs, Paul D. Beloved all have shared portions of human misery. Stamp Paid too is no exception. He carries the burden of his wife-Vashti's degradation. In exchange for his freedom he hands her to be raped by his master's son. No man would ever do this but slaves have no right to manhood and, therefore, Trudier Haris points out "The master's son uses Vashti to assert/declare his manhood; the act simultaneously signals to Joshua that he, a slave, can never be a man."[7] This incident degrades Stamp Paid but fails to dehumanise him. He asserts himself and strives for something more constructive. He ferries escaped slaves to the free territories of Ohio to make his life meaningful. After eighteen years like Paul D. he too reaches Sethe's house and narrates his woe to Paul D. In a way his narrative calls Sethe and Paul D. to open up and thus combined together the narratives of Sweet Home runaways become the story of Sethe—"a story not to pass on" yet cannot be held back and so flows in the pages of Toni Morrison's *Beloved.*

After discussing *Beloved* as a slave narrative the question that comes to our mind is observed by Gates in the introduction to *The Slave Narratives.*

> Once slavery was abolished, no need existed for the slave to write himself (or herself) into the human community through the action of first person narration. As Fredrick Douglas in 1855 succinctly put the matter, the free human being "cannot see things in the same light with the slave, because he does not and cannot look from the same point from which the slave does."[8]

But deliberately and consciously remembering the past helps in giving meaning to the present individual and collective life. Slavery is a part of their ethnic experience and retelling and re-examining of it especially by the New Negro women would help "to create and keep alive the breast of the black men [...] and to fight with dauntless courage, unrelenting zeal and intelligent vision for the attainment of the stature of a full man; a free race and a new world."[9]

Toni Morrison's narratives sing the praise of black art, music, folklore in order to celebrate black identity with the intention to rescue the qualities of resistance, excellence and integrity which helped them to survive slavery and could now be useful to the present growing up generation of Blacks whereas Laxman Gaikwads autobiographical novel, exhibits the anger and shame of being branded as thugs and portrays how the communal identity given to them by the traditional structures of exploitation is the main cause of their exclusion from the share of nation's prosperity and progress. Gaikwad probes deeply for the origin of oppression, victimization and social order and through his narrative makes a plea for Dalits to be treated as human beings rather than objects of disgust.

The slavery experience in America and the experiences of maimed and marginalised Dalits have much in common. Both are regarded as outcasts, both are deprived of minimal means of living, both are exploited and oppressed. The Dalit as Professor Narang stated in his keynote address at a seminar are a nation within a nation and to Gaikwad this concept is a negative one and therefore he constructs his narrative within a negative space. The very opening lines of the novel exhibit his urge to create space both for his narrative and his community. The novel ends with a sad realization that his struggle for emancipation would be a never ending one. Gaikwad realises that his rebellion cannot be sustained without a hope of victory and it is difficult to achieve individuality and full humanity in a manipulative society but not to negotiate that state of tension and negation is to accept self-hatred.

The first half of the novel deals with the writer's childhood memories. It is a horrifying account of the subhuman condition under which the members of this community in the interior district of Latur in Maharashtra live. The use of the local Marathi dialect matches perfectly with the experiences, and the life portrayed appears to be very Horrible. How could one live like this, is the response the narrative arouses. There is an account of the little hut in which Gaikwad lived. When one moves into the interior of a very small hut one finds that it houses goats, dogs, seven members and only one blanket shared between a dog, the writer's brother, the writer and lices. They fight cold with warm urine provided by the goat nearby—"The lamb pissed and the hot water tricked under our bodies. We wished lambs kept pissing so that it warded off the chilly feelings" (*The Branded:* 11). His people do not even know what a proper meal is. They thrive on dead rats in the fields, stray pets and left over thrown in the dustbins. There is a humorous and pathetic account of the writer's confusion when he is invited to dine with a rich friend. He had never seen a big steel plate, with so many bowls. Eatables served were beyond his wildest fancy and he is confused as to what to eat and how to eat it. It was impossible for him at that stage of his life to understand the ways of the rich. He had no sense of socially acceptable behaviour because he had been denied primary socialisation. This and series of other incidents in the novel are powerfully suggestive of Laxman's poverty which is a glaring social reality that cannot be ignored. However, in spite of all odds against him he gets an opportunity to receive little formal education. The account of his difficulties in receiving education is movingly portrayed. Gaikwad's dauntless courage is exhibited in his determination to struggle for betterment without resorting to the means of living adopted by his community. It is in school after having read the stories of Buddha and Mahaveer that he senses great upheaval and surging energy which in turn gives voice to Laxman. He becomes a social activist determined to struggle against injustice and the last part of the novel provides a detailed account of the atrocities and injustice inflicted by the highbrows police and politicians against his community. People in position listen to him and even make a show of sympathizing with his cause but behind the back these very people try hard to beat his cause.

Frustrated by his activities as a social worker Gaikwad turned to writing with a definite political intention. In order to strengthen his mission he wanted a larger section of his country to take notice of this plight of his community and rethink about them in humanistic terms. The shocking reality of the sub human kind of life forced upon them is expressed forcefully and honestly in *The Branded* a book that claims very little literary merit totally lacking the finish and richness of Toni Morrison's novel yet succeeds in leaving a powerful impact on the readers. It is this quality that has made this novel an important social document. It has won Sahitya Academy Award in 1988 and has been translated both in Hindi and English.

In the present Indian context novels like *The Branded* have a great and significant role to play. The tragedy of these "unequal Indians"[10] needs to be voiced and as Dhirubhai L. Sheth, political sociologist observes "Historically marginalised population, like say the Dalits, always existed in India. But today, the types, numbers, degrees of marginalisation and neglect have increased manifold and taken on grim proportions."[11] The stories of these maimed, marginalised, weakest citizen who are faceless, voiceless and geographically segregated fellow human need to be told. They need committed writers like Gaikwad and Toni Morrison to give their woe a voice. Sara Blackman in her review of Sula comments:

> Toni Morrison is far too talented to remain only a marvelous recorder of the black side of provincial American life. If she is to maintain the large and serious audience she deserves, she is going to have to address a riskier contemporary reality than this beautiful but nevertheless distant novel. And if she does this, it seems to me that she might easily transcend that early and unintentionally limiting classification "black woman writer" and take her place among the most serious, important and talented American novelist working.[12]

According to Sara Blackman Toni Morrison should wipe out the label of black writer to become universal writer. However, Toni Morrison has proved her worth and won the Nobel Prize. In her interview to Robert B. Stepto she said she refuses to bow down to politics of publication and has a firm conviction that literature on black has a great future, "lot of people are interested, not just for research purposes as you know, but in terms of gem, theme, the juice of fiction."[13] This humanitarian zeal of both Gaikwad and Toni Morrison enables them to transcend the boundaries of caste and class and meaningfully contribute to the great humanistic tradition of world literature.

NOTES

1. Toni Morrison, *The Bluest Eye* (New York: Pocket Books, 1972), 18.
2. ——., *Sula* (Great Britain: Triad Paperback, 1982), 52.
3. ——., *Beloved* (New York: Penguin Books, 1988), 200. All subsequent references to Beloved are to this edition and have been incorporated in the text itself and will be referred to as *Beloved.*
4. Laxman Gaikwad, *The Branded* (New Delhi: Sahitya Academi

1998), vii. Subsequent references to the novel are to this edition and have been incorporated in the text itself and will be referred to as *The Branded.*

5. Marilyn Sanders Mobley, "A Different Remembering: Memory, History, and Meaning in *Beloved,*" in *Toni Morrison : Critical Perspectives Past and Present,* ed. Henry Louis Gates, Jr., and K.A. Appiah (New York: Amistad, 1993), 363.
6. Roberta Rubenstein, "Pariahs and Community," *Toni Morrison,* ed. Gates, 143-44.
7. Trudier Harris, "Escaping Slavery but Not its Images," in *Toni Morrison,* ed. Gates, 331.
8. Henry Louis Gates, "Introduction" in *The Slaves Narrative* ed. Charles T. Davies and Henry Louis Gates, Jr. (New York: OUP, 1985), xiii.
9. Quote from an entry in the monthly symposium organised by *The Messenger* and printed in its issue on July 5, 1923, 757.
10. The phrase "Unequal Indian" is the title on the cover page of a weekly magazine *Outlook,* August 2, 2001.
11. *Outlook* 54.
12. Sara Blackburn, "You Still Can't Go Home Again," *New York Times Review,* December 30, 1973, 3.
13. Toni Morrison, "Intimate Thing in Place" Conversation with Robert B. Stepto printed in *Toni Morrison,* ed. Gates 394.

17

Radha-Krishna Love-Lore: A Quest For True Love in The Poetry of Kamala Das

VANDANA SHARMA

> "Love is the only ritual I believe in,
> it makes everything legitimate."[1]

Kamala Das or better known as Kamala Suraiyya after her conversion to Islam in December 1999, has always generated controversy amongst readers and writers. Her frank outpourings have often jolted the reader who wonders as to why she is so bold in her writings. Her writings encompass a woman's longings, hopes and fears. Love is a pivotal point round which the writings of Kamala Das revolves.

Prior to her conversion to Islam, Kamala Das to her credit had a corpus of literary works, written both in English and Malayalam. The present paper is, however, an analysis of her earlier writings.

Kamala Das's poetic expression represents the sensibility and sensitivity of a modern Indian woman. She chooses to write freely on the trials and tribulations of the woman who is struggling hard to create a niche for herself in the male-dominated society. Being a modern woman, Kamala Das is aware of her rights and privileges, and this consciousness makes her defiant against the irrational conventions and customs of society.

The urge of establishing her own identity and freedom makes Kamala Das stand apart from the rest of her contemporaries. She deals with the subjects that have never been discussed before. Her works are replete with the study of love and sex. In a bold and assertive voice, she writes profusely about her own experiences. Her frank and confessional outbursts give a new dimension to her poetry. Her candid revelations sometimes jar and jolt the reader who is not accustomed to such expressions. Despite all this, Kamala Das is on her path of exploring her self through self-introspection and self-analysis. She freely gives vent to her emotions, feelings, and thoughts. 'I' or the study of self is a predominant factor in her poetry.

Literary works of Kamala Das are more or less autobiographical in form. She unravels her experiences including those of love; right from her childhood to the age of maturity.

The present paper is an attempt to study Kamala Das's concept of love from the spiritual point of view as discussed in her poems.

The poetry of Kamala Das projects her intense craving for love. It seems that she has an intense desire to love and to be loved. The poet has admitted that love is the main theme of her poems. In her own words:

> Love is beautiful, whatever
> four-lettered name the
> puritans call it by. It is
> the fore state of paradise.
> It is the only pastime that
> involves the soul.[2]

Love for Kamala Das means not only physical union of bodies but also of minds and the souls. Without emotional and spiritual fulfilment, love is merely a "skin-communicated thing."[3] She wants to experience love to its very depth. One of the critics writes:

> Her poetic corpus configurates
> an inner voyage, an aware-
> ness beyond 'Skin's lazy
> hungers,' to the hidden soul.
> It enacts her quest, an

exploration into her self and
seeking of her identity.[4]

Kamala Das does not ignore the physical aspect of love. Sex remains an outer garb for her inner world of emotions and feelings. She does not experience eternal bliss in her marital relationship. This disappoints her but she continues her search for true love. Her unending and untiring search for love, takes her from pole to pole. She steps out of the legal orbit of marriage but every time physical pleasure alone brings only frustration and disappointment. In spite of such failures, Kamala Das is still hopeful of experiencing eternal love. She continues her search with a relentless fervour without a feeling of shame or guilt:

[...] Even my soul,
I thought, must send its roots somewhere,
and, I loved his body without shame
on winter evenings as cold winds
chuckled against the window panes.[5]

It appears that the poet is obsessed with the theme of love. She thinks of love as a beautiful thing and a 'Thapasaya.' She begins to identify her relationship with the love-lore of Radha-Krishna, and seeks the image of Krishna in her lovers. For her, Krishna is the ultimate lover. In this context she reveals:

I grew up reading Geetha-Govinda,
about Radha-Krishna. Which
Hindu girl has not been interested
in Krishna, the great lover? So to
us Krishna has not been vulgar
at all. To us, it has just been normal.[6]

The poet aspires for true and ideal love that bounds Radha and Krishna. At times she imagines herself to be Radha who is waiting for her lover Krishna. Kamala Das tries to justify her illicit love affairs by giving mythical frame to her love.

Some of the poems of Kamala Das depict emotional and spiritual facets of love. For instance in the poem *Radha*, Kamala Das delineates the feelings and ecstasy of Radha:

The long waiting
Had made their bond so chaste,
and all the doubting
And the reasoning
So that in his first true embrace,
she was girl
And virgin crying
Everything in me
Is melting, even the hardness at the core
O Krishna, I am melting, melting, melting,
Nothing remains but
You.[7]

The poet envisages love as a medium which unites the souls. Radha loved Krishna but was married to another man. However, she continued to love Krishna. The two lovers used to meet on the banks of the river Jamuna. For the first time when Krishna embraced Radha she felt as if her entire self began to melt. In Krishna's arms Radha felt that her own identity was dissolving away. Her individuality was lost and there was only Krishna—her eternal lover. In a disguised form, she feels herself merging with her lover. Her 'self' seems to be taken away under the spell of her lover.

Kamala Das admires and adores Krishna and her interest in the mythic lover grows stronger. She reaffirms her faith by saying:

But illogical that I am from
birth onwards. I have always
thought of Krishna as my mate.
When I was a child I used
to regard him as my only
friend. When I became an
adult, I thought of him as
my lover [...]. Now in middle
age, having no more desire
unfulfilled I think of Krishna
as my friend, like me grown
wiser with years, a house-holder
and a patriarch. And illogically

again, I believe that in death
I might come face to face with
Him.[8]

From the above lines it appears that Kamaia Das has always had one image in her mind—Krishna. Her mind and soul have always lived with Krishna.

In another poem *Krishna*, the poet expresses her intense desire to merge with Krishna for emotional solace and eternal bliss. She states:

Your body is my prison, Krishna,
I cannot see beyond it.
Your darkness blinds me,
Your love words shut out the
wise world's din.[9]

The poet feels herself captive in the body of Krishna, which is the cell where she feels secure. His presence both, mental and physical, overshadows her identity. Her journey of life ends when she is united with Krishna. Under the spell and charm of Krishna, she is unable to hear the voices of the world and human world appears meaningless to her. There is only Krishna all-around her.

The poem *The Maggots* signifies the grief of Radha. After her marriage, Radha has to perform her social duty of being a traditional wife to her husband. She has to conceal her feelings and love for Krishna and has to fulfil all wishes of her husband. The grief of Radha is portrayed vividly in the following lines:

At sunset on the river bank, Krishna
loved her for the last time and left.
That night in her, husband's arms
Radha felt
so dead that he asked what is
wrong do you mind my kisses love,
and she said no, not at all, but
thought, what is it to the corpse
if the maggots nip?[10]

The last meeting with Krishna leaves Radha depressed and sad. However, she does not allow her pain to be seen and accepts her husband's love. She remains calm and passive. Her husband loves and kisses her but she gives no indication of her sadness. Rather she feels that it doesnot matter if her husband loves her physically because her soul is devoted and dedicated to Krishna. She finds herself a corpse in her husband's arms. Her soul is intact and physical rupture is insignificant to her. Nothing happens to a dead body when small worms bite it.

Kamala Das is very unhappy when she does not find solace in her husband's arms. Lack of emotional fulfilment in her marital relationship leaves her depressed and dejected and she turns to other men for gratification. Soon she realises that ultimate happiness and tranquility lie in being united with Krishna.

The theme of love is further discussed in the poem, *Radha-Krishna.* The poet celebrates the freedom of the two lovers. Once free from the human bondage the two souls can be united easily. Nobody can stop them from meeting with one another. The two lovers want to rise above the physical trappings so that their souls may be free for the unification. The following lines convey the feelings of the two lovers:

> This becomes from this hour
> Our river and this old Kadamba
> tree, ours alone, for our homeless
> souls to return someday,
> to hang like bats
> from its pure physicality.[11]

The two lovers are hopeful that one-day they might get an abode where the two can live peacefully and happily.

The title of the poem *Ghanashyam* describes the poet's intense love for Krishna. The persona of the poem addresses Krishna with great joy and excitement.

> Ghanashyam,
> You have like a koel built your
> Nest in the harbour of my heart.
> My life, until now, a sleeping jungle,
> Is at last astir with music.[12]

When Radha meets Krishna she gets intoxicated with life. Krishna enlivens her life. She begins to love Krishna emotionally and spiritually. Their love becomes an ideal relationship. This relationship is an ideal example for Kamala Das's theory of love. She feels that ultimate bliss can be achieved only in emotional and spiritual union. Critic A.N. Dwivedi comments on this aspect of love:

> It is this framework (Radha-Krishna love-lore) that saves her, in some degree, from the charges of obscenity and promiscuity, otherwise her poetry is replete with shocking and unorthodox details about love and marriage and sex.[13]

NOTES AND REFERENCES

1. Priya Pathiyan, "Love is the only ritual I believe in" an article on Kamala Das, *The Sunday Review,—The Times of India,* April 21, 2001.
2. Kamala Das, "Obscenity and Literature," *Weekly Round Table,* April 1972.
3. Kamala Das, *Only The Soul Knows How To Sing, selections from Kamala Das* (Kerala: D.C. Books, 1996), 89.
4. Hari Mohan Prasad and Chakradhar Prasad Singh (ed.), *Indian Poetry in English* (New Delhi, Sterling Publishers Pvt. Ltd., 1986), 35.
5. *Only The Soul Knows How To Sing* 99.
6. Kamala Das, "I believe" *Savy* Magazine, Dec. 1990, 17.
7. *Only The Soul Knows How To Sing* 63.
8. Kamala Das. "Sex, Mindless Surrender or Humming Fiesta," *Femina*: June 6, 1977, 19.
9. *Only The Soul Knows How To Sing* 67.
10. *Only The Soul Knows How To Sing* 42.
11. *Only The Soul Knows How To Sing* 104.
12. *Only The Soul Knows How To Sing* 94.
13. A.N. Dwivedi, *Kamala Das and Her Poetry* (New Delhi: Doaba House, 1983), 37.

18

A Post-colonial Reading of Anita Nair's *Ladies Coupe*

INDIRA NITYANANDAM

Post-colonialism can be seen "as a theoretical resistance to the mystifying amnesia of the colonial aftermath. It is a disciplinary project devoted to the task of revisiting, remembering and crucially interrogating the colonial past" (Gandhi 4). As it is essential to return to the colonial scene, there is constantly a relationship of reciprocal antagonism between colonizer and colonized. We are still in the process of choosing the term that best expresses this relationship. There are three options—First, the hyphenated 'post-colonialism'—a decisive temporal marker of the decolonising process (others question the implied chronological separation between colonialism and its aftermath). Second, 'post-colonialism'—the unbroken term seems to be more sensitive to the long history of colonial consequences as according to them the post-colonial condition is inaugurated with the onset rather than the end of colonial occupation. Third, post-coloniality or 'the post-colonial' which has an existential resonance and not a notion of academic dogma.

It is with post-colonialism that for the first time the non-West is placed at the center of the dominant discourse. All post-colonial writing is writing produced in the former colonies—it may not be resistant or oppositional and hence not necessarily writing back. The study of colonial discourse has "blossomed into a garden where the marginal can speak and be spoken, even spoken for" (Spivak 56). It is important to remember that all post-colonial writing is not the same even when they are all born out of the colonial experience. Beyond their special and distinctive regional characteristics, they have emerged in their present form out of the experience of colonization and asserted themselves by foregrounding the tension with the imperial power and by emphasizing their differences from the assumptions of the imperial centre. It is this which makes them distinctly post-colonial.

National independence may lead to a desire for collective historical amnesia—a desire for a total breakaway or a radical separation from the colonizer. However, this post-colonial dream of discontinuity is unrealistic because the colonial aftermath actually calls for an ameliorative and therapeutic remembering and recalling of the colonial past. This is similar to Lyotard's psychoanalytic procedure of 'anamnesis' or analysis in which patients are urged to elaborate their current problems by freely associating apparently inconsequential details of past situations. By this process a complex project of historical and psychological recovery is set into motion. Hence, thinking about the past is one essential aspect of any post-colonial approach. In fact, Homi Bhabha suggests that memory is the necessary and sometimes hazardous bridge between colonialism and the question of cultural identity. It is a painful remembering, a putting together of the dismembered past to make sense of the trauma of the present. It is necessary to release offending memories from their captivity. Colonial aftermath combines 'vedrangung'-repression of memory and 'verwerfung'-repudiation of memories. The theoretical remembering of the colonial condition has to fulfil two corresponding functions—(a) A simple disinterment or digging up of unpalatable memories which seeks to uncover the overwhelming and lasting violence of colonization and (b) A reconciliatory attempt to make the hostile and the antagonistic past more familiar and, therefore, more approachable.

Thus, it is clear that post-coloniality has to be made to concede its part or complicity in the terrors and errors of its own past. There is an ambivalent and symbiotic relationship between the colonizer and the colonized. As Memmi argues, the lingering residue of colonization will decompose only if, and when, we are willing to acknowledge the reciprocal behaviour of the two partners. There is a perverse mutuality between the oppressor and the oppressed—"the desire of the colonizer for the colonized is obvious and transparent but the inverse longing of the colonized is difficult to understand" (45). In literature, the term post-colonial suggests de-linking from a centralist undertone and instead prioritises de-centering, plurality, hybridity and a dismantling of authority. It suggests an attempt to reclaim an autonomous and free identity. It recreates an identity for the colonized. Post-colonial literatures display an increasing awareness of the close alliance between discourse and power. Said has also put forward the argument that postcolonialism should reconsider the significance of all other liberationist activities like feminism etc.

In discussing post-colonialism, one has to realize the crucial function of language as a medium of power. Hence, post-colonial writing has to define itself by seizing the language of the centre and replacing it in a discourse fully adapted to the colonized place. This has to be done by two distinct processes. First, abrogation or denial of the privilege of English which involves a rejection of metropolitan power. Second, appropriation and reconstitution of the language of the centre, a process of capturing and moulding the language to new usages—marking a separation from the site of colonial privilege.

Indeed, post-colonial literatures have now emerged from heterogeneous linguistic sources comprised of indigenous languages (oral as well as written) which colonizing languages have attempted to stifle. Post-colonial writers have been acutely conscious of the formative, political and elusive power of language. Their work has engaged the readers in complex cultural narratives, sharpening awareness of the inextricable relationship between language and politics.

Post-colonialism has led to a growth of anti-colonial nationalism—an offshoot of postcolonial nation states, themselves steeped in authoritarian and chauvinist boundaries. Independent states, in their anti-Western focus, often deflect attention from their own post-colonial, structural hierarchies.

Said points out that the intellectual stirrings of post-colonialism can be properly realized only when nationalism becomes more critical of itself and when it proves itself capable of directing attention to the abused rights of all classes. Thus, post-colonialism should attempt to produce a more critical self-reflexive account of cultural nationalism. Hence in Dalit writings or women's writing or any literature produced by the marginalized, the shades of colonialism are still clearly seen. The Third-World woman cannot be seen as a single, monolithic subject.

Post in post-colonialism should signify changes in the power structure after the official end of colonialism. But post-colonial discourse does betray the colonial influence even in the genre of the novel. *Ladies Coupe* (*LC*) is the story of six women who meet, purely by chance, on a short train journey. The protagonist Akhila—"Akhilandeswari. Mistress of all worlds. Master of none" (*LC* 84) hopes to find answers to many of the questions that have been troubling her, but realizes like the protagonists of Shashi Deshpande's novels that there can be no pat answers, that no one can teach her how to live her life, that she cannot model her life on the lives of others. "It occurred to Akhila suddenly that she was doing it all wrong. She was treating other people's lives as though they were how-to books that would help her find clear-cut answers to what she needed to do next" (*LC* 40). In the postcolonial scenario, this is important because the homogenizing nature of the modern concept of nation may subsume individual aspirations and expectations. She is an individual with her own aspirations and ideas. Yet, eating an egg seems to be the only self-asserting and self-fulfilling action that she seems to have the courage to execute for the greater part of her life. Even this is done away from the prying and proselytizing eyes and attitudes of the members of her own family. It is only when Katherine leaves that Akhila begins to cook and eat eggs in her mother's kitchen. "All of Akhila's wondrous explorations and magical discoveries were locked within the fragile shell of an egg" (*LC* 90). Years later when she decides to begin eating eggs after moving into her own flat, Padma sits in judgment saying, "We are Brahmins. We are not supposed to. It is against the norms of our caste" (*LC* 161-61).

This attempt at levelling all forms of difference may be a dangerous development for the marginalized in any newly independent country because the Empire may then be replaced by an equally autocratic nation state regime. The women in these societies have to continue to wage their own battles even in the post-colonial period.

After her father's sudden and untimely death, Akhila takes on the entire responsibility of her family. Anita Nair probably hints at the family's easy acceptance of her as the head of the family—a place traditionally reserved for the patriarch in both the colonial and post-colonial periods. In spite of being the bread winner and hence occupying the centrist position, she still continues to remain on the periphery because she is still seen as a woman and her needs are never considered important enough to take precedence over the needs of the other members of the family. As the younger sister Padma grows up, her marriage is planned but no one seems to think that Akhila too has her needs. Akhila continued to be the head of the family. "Someone who would chart and steer the course of the family's destiny to safe shores" (*LC* 76). Akhila continues to tolerate the invasion of her space and privacy even when Padma and family move in to live with her.

It is indeed ironic that the woman who took on the responsibility of the entire family years ago is not considered capable of looking after herself even at the age of 45. Can a woman live alone? What will society say? Ask your brothers for their opinion before taking a decision—is the advice given to her. The reactions of Narsi and Padma reveal the attitudes of society towards a single woman. Like the white man's burden during the colonial period, this is used in the post-colonial period to limit the freedom to think and act of the colonized or the marginalized. Nair uses the opportunity to delineate the callousness and selfish nature of human beings while making a clear statement about society's double standards. In this post-colonial situation, the man is the colonizer and the woman the colonized as we see in the case of Ebenezer-Margaret or Jagdeesh-Prabha Devi. "He will pet you and cosset you at first, for after all you are appealing to the male in him to protect and safeguard. But it will be only a matter of days before he turns into a tyrant and will want to control your every thought" (*LC* 188). Like the colonizer earlier the male ensures that the female, like the colonized, becomes calcified in her opinion about her lack of self-sufficiency. She begins to depend on the male and accepts the fact that she cannot live alone. As Prabha Devi puts it, "show him you are incapable of doing anything beyond the periphery of your home and he will manage your life, from sending postal orders to balancing cheque books to booking railway tickets to managing household expenses" (*LC* 188). As Fanon has stated, colonialism does not aim at killing the native culture because it wants to perpetuate the agony of the colonized. These women are aware that they are not helpless but yet are marginalized.

Margaret Shanthi is another example of how women are dominated upon by male power—the powerless are like the colonized who fail to see and appreciate their true worth. When she marries Ebenezer Paulraj, she has made the perfect choice according to her family. Her brother-in-law voices their feelings when he says, "We couldn't have found a better match for you if we had looked ourselves" (*LC* 102). Societal expectations far outweigh personal needs and so Shanthi negates herself again and again. From an ambitious and brilliant student who wants to chart out a career on her own, she becomes a dutiful wife to Ebenezer who rouses fear in everyone around him. Time and again, she silences her aspirations in order to be what Ebenezer wants her to be. Like the colonized, she seems convinced that it is for her own good. And so, she begins to want only what he wanted. She decided to become a teacher instead of working on her doctorate, she cut her hair short, she stopped going to church every Sunday, eating bhelpuri outside and finally agrees even to abort her child though she knows that her religion forbids it. As usual, he takes the decisions and "I (Shanthi) let his voice smooth away my fears. He was Ebe. My Ebe. He was right. He was always right" (*LC* 109). And then anger envelopes her as she realizes that even in the most important decisions of her life, she only toes his line. She wakes up to this fact and plans her own strategy to prove her strength. Much like the colonized, Margaret Shanthi develops the ability to work for her own independent identity.

Ladies Coupe is not an indictment of the institution of marriage as we see a closeness in couples like Akhila's parents or Janaki and Prabhakar. Instead it stresses on the need for mutual respect and understanding as well as self-respect. It addresses problems of female sexuality as in the case of Prabha Devi who is finally able to decide to live life on her own terms and gives expression to her needs and desires and finally, chalks out her own space.

As in the case of the colonized here too there are divisions among the women themselves. Most of them lack the ability to accept and appreciate the achievements of a successful woman—whether she is married like Karpagam's mother or single like Akhila. Karpagam's mother taught dance but Akhila's mother considered it demeaning to use her voice and earn some money by teaching music. When Akhila meets Karpagam after a span of twenty years, "Akhila realized with shame that while she had in the manner of a docile water-buffalo wallowed in self-pity, allowing parasites to feast on her, Karpagam had gone ahead and learnt to survive" (*LC* 202). Again, it is Karpagam who is able to instill a sense of self-worth in Akhila which makes her decide to live her life on her own terms and not be dictated to by other members of the family who are actually dependent on her.

The female body becomes the site of violence in the case of the rape of Marikolanthu. Like the violence unleashed by the colonizer on the powerless colonized, she has to face physical brutality as well as mental torture when left to fend for herself. With his brute strength, Murugesan attacks her and she is left helpless. She is different from the other women in the coupe because her experiences are far more painful.

As an alternative type of female bonding, Nair introduces lesbianism—between Misses K and V and later between Sujata Akka and Marikolanthu. In the latter case, the female bonding is all the more important because it breaks away from class distinctions. The colonized (women) become one against the males.

All post-colonial texts have within them energies to subvert the repressive forces of colonial ideas. However, it becomes important to consider all literatures of these countries as post-colonial writing instead of only the literatures in English.

WORKS CITED

Fanon, F., *The Wretched of the Earth* 3rd edn. Trans. Constance Farrington, Penguin, Harmondsworth, 1990.

Gandhi, Leela, *Postcolonial Theory.* New Delhi: OUP, 1998.

Indira C.T. and Meenakshi Shivram, ed. *Post-Coloniality.* New Delhi: Vikas, 1999.

Juneja, Om P., *Post Colonial Novel.* New Delhi: Creative, 1995.

Memmi, A., *Dominated Man: Notes Towards a Portrait.* London: Orion Press, 1968.

Nair, Anita, *Ladies Coupe.* India: Penguin, 2001.

Spivak, G., *Outside in the Teaching Machine.* New York: Routledge, 1993.

19

The Changing Pattern of Man-Woman Relationship in Modern Indian English Novels—1980-2000

JOYA CHAKRAVARTY

Man-Woman Relationship in modern times has undergone a sea change. Formerly, the Indian woman was a typical product of tradition, destined to become a shadow of her husband, although some palliatives had been adroitly devised to keep her ego satisfied—for instance, no religious ceremony could be considered complete unless the wife sat by the husband to perform the religious rituals. Moreover, at the time of weddings, there were certain customary ceremonies exclusively to be conducted and performed by women.

In the agricultural sector, women did enjoy certain privileges by their entitlement to give away food grains and other household possessions to labourers in return for the work done. But as stated above, all these were sheer palliatives and consolatory expedients. With the change in the socio-political scene after independence and at the call of Gandhi and his followers, women started enjoying greater importance, and their role in the freedom struggle became quite significant. With the advancement of education women started taking up jobs in addition to their household duties. However, the upshot of all these changed conditions was that women started realising their individuality and learnt to establish their separate entities not only in society but also in domestic circles. This social and economic uplift in their status resulted in a change in their behaviour pattern. Their attitude towards sex and sexuality also underwent a notable change. Now there was more of self-expression and a far less inhibited assertion of their inner volitions in their sexual roles. All this was unimaginable in pre-independent India.

In modern Indian English novels, writers like Anita Desai, Shashi Deshpande, Upmanyu Chatterjee, Amitav Ghosh, Arundhati Roy, Manju Kapoor have tried to underline these significant changes by creating illustrative situations and characters in different context. The additional charm of these novels also resides in the graph that they have tried to chart out in the advancement of women from tradition to modernity.

Man-woman relationship in modern Indian English novels has acquired varied dimensions. The hidden meanings and the sexual innuendoes in the dialogues point to a rapidly changing society in which conventional values are crumbling. Social norms and conventions have now been thrown to the winds. The modern Indian man and the modern Indian woman have now become acquisitive—the age of "go-getters" has now set in. The novels of the writers mentioned above reveal the flux in the world around them and there is an ease about the mixing of the real and the fantastical. The novels focus on issues like marriage, commercialisation, destitution, communalism, crisis of the individual, alienation and a general dilution of values once held dear. Western influence and the westernization of Indian society, especially in the upper classes stand in sharp contrast to the traditionalism of the middle and lower classes.

The narrative technique of these novelists do not follow the conventional format, *i.e.*, there is no proper/conventional beginning, middle or end. Modern Indian English novels employ a multiplicity of forms. At times, however, there is a breakdown of form or there is a combination of different forms. This diversity points to the vitality of the form, its dynamism and its constant evolution. The writers juggle with time and space and the reader has to continually adjust himself to the different time frames. Arundhati Roy's book *The God of Small Things* highlights this practice very effectively.

From times immemorial, throughout the world, there has

been a fixed image of man and woman in the minds of the readers. Traditionally, the image of woman has been what men have thought it should be. A "good" woman is one who is meek, docile, passive, obedient, virtuous, humble, kind and self-sacrificing. A "bad" woman was one who was bold, adventurous, active, articulate, intelligent and questioning—conduct of such a woman was not appreciated by society—a society which was shaped by men who laid down the norms of behaviour. Thus the image of the good or bad woman has been fixed in our minds and this has shaped the course of most of the literatures of the world. This image of woman is found in the cultural attitudes of the world and departure from this has come to stand for the dividing line between tradition and modernity.

Traditionally, men control and inhabit the power structures and they understand the dynamics of economics. Men make and take decisions on property and lay down the rules of morality. They have categorised women into good and bad and have indoctrinated both women and men to such an extent that by and large they have come to accept these categories. Men have thus evolved the dual strategy of control and exclusion.[1]

Women were respected provided they conformed to the norms laid down by society. Sudhir Kakar in *Feminine Identity in India* and in *Intimate Relations observes,* that a woman's status in Indian society is determined by her faithful adherence to the prescribed code of behaviour. The traditional image has both positive and negative connotations. Images restrict a person, hamper freedom and a woman not conforming to the image is either annihilated or denigrated. The modern Indian woman finds herself in a peculiar situation—her freedom to interact with men is hampered by traditions and conventions.

The stereotyped roles of femininity have restricted and obstructed the growth and emancipation of women. This stunting of individual growth and development has brought in its wake a note of anger and bitterness which becomes evident in the portrayals of women characters in the novels of Anita Desai, Nayantara Sahgal, Arundhati Roy and others. The modern Indian writer has questioned the need to accept the image of women as created by men.

In today's world of information technology exclusion or even segregation of women from public life is no longer possible. Novelists have begun to comment on the predicament of the modern Indian woman. Hesitant and slightly unsure of herself, the modern Indian woman struggles for acceptance, both at her workplace and at home. She is, therefore, Janus-faced—one face looks back to the ancient traditional image and the other face looks forward to a whole new world waiting for her to conquer.

For a very long time it has been ingrained in the mind of an Indian woman that marriage is the ultimate goal of her life and her husband's home is her only abode. However, the modern educated Indian woman finds that marriage allows only an outward semblance of freedom. Indian society is still very conventional in its approach to marriage and despite numerous contradictions, husband and wife strive to maintain an outward show of balance and harmony. In the career-graph of man and woman (husband and wife), it is always the woman who must curb her individuality so that her husband's career remains open to a meteoric rise.

The Indian woman has begun to realise that marriage in most cases acts as a deterrent—it is not a loving and equal partnership. Marriage cuts a woman off from the mainstream of life and prevents her from achieving her goals. A successful marriage is supposed to be one where the woman restricts herself to the household affairs. The code of conduct is peculiar—the man is the boss of the house, his every whim has to be catered to. However, outside the household precincts he behaves differently, mixes with his female colleagues on an equal footing and even yields to their whims and fancies. The man will either never discuss his female colleagues with his wife or if he does then it will be to flaunt them before her to prove his macho spirit. Beyond the threshold of her house a woman finds life insecure and confusing due to her hitherto social and cultural seclusion. Whenever women have stepped out of their confines, they have had to struggle against the fixed image of women in the minds of men and women. Moreover, they have had to struggle against prejudices and dual standards prevalent in society. An Indian woman has been either venerated as a goddess or rejected as a siren. The modern Indian woman has to compete against these two extreme images. She is striving to lead the life of a normal human being with normal desires. She does not wish to succumb to the pressures of patriarchy, marginality, and helplessness. In her desire to establish a viable relationship with the people that she works with, the Indian woman must break free from the bondage of conventions and subordination inbuilt in patriarchal societies. An equitable man-woman relationship can only be established if we get rid of the traditional image. Venerating and worshipping a woman only-serves to isolate her from the realities of life.

The changing pattern of man-woman relationship can be traced in the works of Anita Desai, N. Sahgal, A. Roy, Manju Kapoor, U. Chatterjee and Amitav Ghosh. These writers have shown how the modern Indian woman attempts to free herself sexually and domestically from role bondage sanctioned by the past. The male and female characters in these novels try to grapple with their interpersonal problems with or without success; often ending in some kind of a truce. The novelists, like the readers, know that there is no logical analysis of emotion. However, it is interesting to note how certain types of men and certain types of women get along very well. The novelists often focus upon the lack of emotional fulfilment in man-woman relationship. In *The God of Small Things*, Ammu Craves for emotional solace and love but this is denied to her. Her relationship with Velutha gives her carnal satisfaction. Dissatisfaction in marriage may stem from many factors as highlighted by Anita Desai, Shashi Deshpande, Manju Kapoor and U. Chatterjee.

Pre-marital and post-marital liaisons are often depicted by the modern Indian novelists. Upmanyu Chatterjee appears to be very satirical as he analyses human relationships in *The Last Burden* and *Mammories of a Welfare State*. Our lives revolve around relationships in some form or the other. And it is relationships which make all the difference in life. In India, even today, marriages give sanctity to man-woman relationships. However, the writers mentioned above reveal that marriage as an institution has collapsed. Both men and women have become irritable and impatient with each other. As a result they are broken-hearted and emotionally unstable. Finesse, delicacy and refinement seem to have gone away and in their place materialism reigns.

Shorn of the security of joint families (see *The Last Burden*) men and women are learning the tricks of survival rapidly. Television and internet are fast accelerating the loss of innocence that now comes a trifle too early. Consumerism has taken a firm grip on the life styles of urban Indians. "Due to commercialism and consumerism, the I, Me, Mine, syndrome seeps into the home fronts resulting in more heart breaks, discords, separations and broken households."

The novelists therefore, have questioned the very institution of marriage which has now become very acquisitive and utilitarian. In most marriages love takes a back seat and money dominates. Ideal sexual love is only possible in adultery—this seems to be the general impression one gets while reading modern Indian novels in English. Adulterous relationships are neither acquisitive nor utilitarian—the man and the woman gain solace and support, and derive pleasure and happiness in each other's company. Passion can be either virtuous or vicious depending on whether one is pragmatic and utilitarian or happy and contented. Passionate love for one's own wife or husband is all right, but even an indication of passion for a male or a female friend is not accepted by society. In order to maintain a façade of harmony in their married lives, men and women who enter into adulterous relationships often take recourse to the art of dissembling. The novels show the dilemma of such people and the effect of such relationships on their lives.

Indian Writing in English has come of age blossoming into a thriving industry. The trend began with Sahnan Rushdie's *Midnight's Children* (1980) and ever since then a brood of Indo-Anglian writers have arrived on the Indian literary scene. They are the "formidable literary heirs of Rushdie" and they also command respect in London which is the world's literary centre.

Indian writers writing in English have tried to analyse human relationships, the fragile man-woman relationship. Indian society is rapidly changing and this is affecting our day to day life styles. Moreover, in India, the family continues to be the foundation of society and a lot of Indian Writing has the family as its subject. The family as a social unit is dying in the West. But both in India and in the West relationships matter a great deal in our lives. Cracks often appear in relationships because of some upheaval or the other. Writers delineate these cataclysmic changes that are occurring in interpersonal relationship. Writers are also exploring the impact of technological advancement on society. This has directly or indirectly influenced human relationships and the psychology behind them. The changing pattern of man-woman relationship is presented not only in the novels, but also in films and television serials. Bold themes and diverse issues are now being taken up by the media. The mosaic of stories highlight the fact that man-woman relationship is a very complex and subtle issue.

NOTE

1. See Jain, Jasbir and Amina Amin ed. *Margins of Erasure: Purdah in the Subcontinental Novel in English,* Sterling Publishers: Delhi, 1995.

20

Violence Against Women As Represented In Cowasjee and Duggal's "Orphans of the Storm"

POONAM YADAV

15 August, 1947, is a Red letter day in the history of India, as India attained freedom from a three-century-old British oppression on this day. It was apprehended that with the attainment of independence India would regain its lost glory of being called "Golden Bird." But instead of entering into a new era as hoped by everybody it proved to be the beginning of dark days in the history of Indian sub-continent. The destiny of common people was caught between the greed for power of the political leaders and the haste with which the British Government headed by Prime Minister Attlee, finalised the terms for the transfer of power. Mr. V.P. Menon, the then Reforms Commissioner took just four hours to prepare the plan for the division of India which was accepted by the British cabinet in just five minutes.

This lack of foresight in the hasty implementation of a plan that dealt with the fate of India's vast population led to a holocaust. Overnight India was fragmented into a truncated India and a Muslim Pakistan. This division of power and land left a sad and miserable tale of oppression and exploitation in its wake the consequences of which still remain with us. Even by a conservative estimate, ten million people took to the roads; a million did not make their destination. "Partition was a traumatic experience for me. I had gone to Lahore expecting to live there, to become a lawyer or a judge; then to be brutally torn out and never really being able to go back. That was what put me to writing. I wrote 'Train To Pakistan.' I had no intention of becoming a writer, nor any confidence that I would be able to make a living out of it," says the versatile writer, Khushwant Singh in an exclusive interview with Anuradha Roy in '*The Hindu.*' The issue of Partition is so inflammatory even today that T.V. serials like *Tamas* by Bhishm Sahni and *Buniyad* and movies like *Gadar*, based on the incidents of 1947, receive a tremendous response.

The hypocrisy and double facedness of the society are unveiled in times of struggle for power. Partition of India was one such event. The violence the exploitation, the cruelty and the brutal massacre at the time of partition were perpetrated by people themselves against one another and no governmental agency was to be held guilty.

The traumatic events that followed the partition of India have been a major theme with writers. For some a realistic portrayal of communal violence was the most representative aspect of the Partition experience: while others were left wordless. Faiz Ahmed Faiz summed up their disillusionment and his own in *Subh-i-Azadi*:

This pock-marked morn,
This night-stung dawn,
It is not the dawn we'd longed for.

Even in a country like India where people firmly believe that 'God dwells in places where women are worshipped,' there are times when women have repeatedly become victims of human rage. Partition of India was one such event. Though Partition put forth a variety of subject matter, the majority of the writers chose to deal with violence of one kind or another—violence targeted against women, abduction and rape being their favourites. Rekha Pandey considers rape in India "as a male tendency to become genetically programmed in the fight for the survival of the fittest" (*Women and Violence* 143).

Violence against women and the threat of an assault is repeatedly mentioned in all records of partition. Women were, indeed, the worst sufferers is those terror-ridden traumatic days of partition. Undoubtedly, men also suffered but, theirs was a material, mental, and physical suffering. They were fortunate enough as their wounds were reparable and pain forgettable with the passage of time. Apart from the physical sufferings, women suffered losses in terms of self-esteem, self-respect and dignity, each of which left a permanent imprint on their minds. Unlike men their wounds were unhealable.

We get graphic descriptions of physical abuse and mutilation faced by the women in the writings of some writers. But, with some versatile writers the theme of rape resulted in some of the most heart-wrenching stories ever-written. Among these are Kartar Singh Duggal's "Kulsum" and "Pakistan Zindabad," Rajinder Singh Bedi's "Lajwanti," Saadat Hasan Manto's "The Reunion" and Khwaja Ahmad Abbas's "Revenge." Saros Cowasjee and K.S. Duggal in their anthology entitled "Orphans of the Storm" Stories on the Partition of India categorises them as the post-partition stories that relive the mental agony, physical torture and psychological trauma that women had to undergo during these crises-ridden days.

In all these stories except "Pakistan Zindabad"—the women are raped and abducted during the Partition. "The Reunion" by the well-known Pakistani writer, Saadat Hasan Manto is the most horrifying tale about rape. It is a story about a young Muslim girl who has been raped so often that her hands involuntarily move to undo "the cords which kept her *salwar* tied round her waist" even when the doctor asks the girl's father to open the window. The situation in which the father being unaware of the critical condition of his daughter, Sakina gives an exclamation of joy, "She's alive. My daughter is alive" is ironic. The psychological trauma and mental agony of the girl becomes evident from the fact that her subconscious mind has accepted the word 'Open' to mean the 'undoing of her trouser strings.' In a country like India where sexual purity has always been held in high esteem by women and we have examples of women performing 'Johar' in order to safeguard their honour, through this story we come across a tragic situation in which we see that Sakina instead of revolting gets used to it as she has undergone this torture so often.

Kartar Singh Duggal in "Kulsum" illuminates a moment of horror. In this story a young muslim 'hoor' is raped by an old Sikh for she refuses to sexually oblige his young guest, a schoolmaster. Her earlier plea to the schoolmaster, "Marry me first [...]. I beg of you," repeated many times makes it mere touching. As the old man emerges from the hut tying his lungi we find ourselves as speechless and shocked as the girl, Kulsum, "The girl who had begged and pleaded three minutes ago said nothing. She sat silent [...]." The old man is not at all ashamed of his doing, rather he asks the schoolmaster "to go in without fear." While he himself "walked briskly to the neem tree and going behind it, began washing himself," as if water was sufficient enough to wash off the wrong he had done to the innocent girl, Kulsum.

On one hand we have the old man for whom women were merely an object meant for sexual pleasure and for sexually obliging others. For him women had no entity and feelings of their own. On the other hand we have the schoolmaster representing the educated class, who was in no way better than the old man. For him the muslim girl was "a gift to be swallowed whole." When he failed to exploit the girl sexually he "rose in a towering frenzy and strode out of the hut." He very well knew why the old man went into the hut but, he did nothing to stop him and to save the girl. Even he believed that women were objects meant for the gratification of the sexual needs of men. We even come across the most cherished dream of Indian girls. All Indian girls dream of getting married, of having their own small but happy home and of becoming a mother. Similar was the wish of Kulsum. She repeatedly begged the schoolmaster, "marry me first, please. You are young. Marry me and I shall be the mother of your children. The mother of your pearly children. We shall have our own home and our courtyard [...]."

All her dreams were shattered in just three minutes and we see that the girl who first "stood her ground steadfast," now "sat motionless," "her head averted to one side, her vacant gaze resting on the charpoy." The mental torture of the girl, Kulsum who had been betrayed by the old man and who very well knew what the schoolmaster was trying to do, can be well understood by her words, "Don't do it. I beg of you. Don't do it. Marry me first." "I was betrothed to a man of your age." "This old man caught me [...]. He said he would seek a husband for me. Marry me, please."

Khwaja Ahmad Abbas's "Revenge" is a heart touching story of a father craving for vengeance on seeing his daughter stripped, raped and mutilated in front of him. "Whenever he thought of his daughter Janki something snapped in his brain." He wanted to avenge his daughter's mutilation by stabbing a muslim girl "in her naked breasts." Only this would recompense him. He gets his chance in a brothel. The scene we come across in the brothel is undoubtedly melodramatic, but nonetheless moving: "With a lightning stroke his left hand snatched the brassiere." The dagger remained poised in the air. Beneath the brassiere where he was going to stab her, there were no breasts [...] there was nothing—nothing but two horrible round scars!" A single word "Daughter" escapes his lips.

In the post-partition days people looked at each other not as human beings but as Hindus and Muslims. The Hindus wanted to avenge the wrongs done to them in Pakistan by committing atrocities on muslim women: "After all that you suffered in Pakistan here is your chance to enjoy a Pakistani hoor." Similar was the case with the muslims. In both the cases the ultimate sufferers were women. The women were in a miserable plight. They were reduced to the position of mere objects for recompensing some loss or for taking revenge. The lines, "of the Muslims of Delhi some had been killed others had been frightened into running away to Pakistan, and the few that remained never dared to venture out of the purely muslim localities," stands testimony to the tensed and terror-stricken atmosphere that gripped the length and breadth of the country in the post partition days. The cruelty and brutality of the people against each other in those days crossed all limits as the muslim girl in place of breasts had "nothing but two horrible round scars." Rajinder Singh Bedi's "Lajwanti" deals with the predicament of women who were victims of the brutality and cruelty of the rioters. It is a heart-touching and moving tale of the women who carry their sufferings and miseries beyond a particular time and space in history.

In all these stories of the post-partition period—Kartar Singh Duggal's "Kulsum," Saadat Hasan Manto's "The Reunion," Khwaja Ahmad Abbas's "Revenge" and Rajinder Singh Bedi's "Lajwanti"—we find an absolute objectification of the female. "Whether she is something to be possessed, guarded, looted, assaulted or even rescued, she remains completely as 'object,' the 'other.' In these stories one doesn't find many choices offered to the female and even when she is given a choice there is nothing to choose from among equally painful alternatives."

WORKS CITED

Abbas, Khwaja Ahmad, *Revenge,* Cowasjee & Duggal 14-23.

Bedi, Rajinder Singh, *Lajwanti,* Cowasjee & Duggal 67-78.

Cowasjee, Saros & Duggal, K.S. (ed.) *Orphans of the Storm.* Stories on the Partition of India, UBSPD, New Delhi, 1995.

Duggal, K.S., *Kulsum and Pakistan Zindabad.* Cowasjee & Duggal 94-103.

Manto, Saadat Hasan, *The Reunion.* Cowasjee & Duggal 154-57.

Pandey, Rekha, "Women and Violence" in J. Jain (ed.) *Gender and Narrative.* Rawat Publications, 2002.

Rathore, Ila, "Gender Psyche and the Politics of Power in Partition Literature" in J. Jain (ed.) *Gender and Narrative.* Rawat Publications, 2002.

Singh, Khushwant, "An interview given to Anuradha Roy's in *The Hindu* 3 March 2002.

21

NARRATING INDIANNESS: GITA MEHTA'S *A RIVER SUTRA*

SHUBHSHREE

"Was it worth so much pain to discover something so obvious?" exclaims the narrator of *A River Sutra* disbelievingly at the end of the novel. To his query the enigmatic. Professor Shankar ironically remarks, "Don't you know the soul must travel through eighty-four thousand births in order to become a man?" (281). Gita Mehta thus makes us travel centuries in order to re-interpret what it means to be a man specially in a country where the past lives on into the present although obscured and mystified unrecognizably. Through a device of loosely stitching together each chapter end to end by having a different character from one continue into the next—but no further, Mehta presents the whole spectrum of class, culture and religion that is India. But she does not stop here but goes beyond to encompass the world at large. One can pertinently ask, then why India? She explains, "you stand on geography as a writer. Even if you're writing about Superman, you have to invent a planet for him to come from; you can't write in a void [...]." Most importantly, perhaps, Mehta chooses this subcontinent to be 'the planet' as the backdrop for her stories to move against, because it is the cradle of her own being.

Not only because she hails from India, is the daughter of Biju Patnaik who was an Indianist, a great freedom fighter during India's struggle for Independence, but because as a writer she is drawn to India by a powerful force. She confesses in one of her interviews:

> "India is a place where world and times are colliding with a huge velocity: we're putting satellites into space, and we have bullock carts; there's the constant tension and contradiction of immense sophistication and an almost premedieval way of life [...]."

All this indeed makes India fascinating and it has fascinated Mehta in more ways than one as we can see from her varied writing. Her first book *Karma Cola: Marketing the Mystic East* (1979), took a sardonic look at the Western belief that spiritual enlightenment could be acquired by hopping a jet to India and finding the nearest guru. Her next book, *Raj* (1989) encircled the fifty years preceding Indian Independence. The era is looked at through the fictitious Jaya Singh, the daughter and then the wife of Maharajas who ruled two of India's nominally independent kingdoms. Her latest work *Snakes and Ladders* is a compilation of essays on Modern India. Mehta becomes a camera through which the reader can see her native land.

A River Sutra (1993) blends Indian mythology with a simple storyline concerning a disenchanted bureaucrat learning about life, while attempting to escape from it, from six pilgrims travelling to the Narmada, a sacred river. Initially the river was conceived as the protagonist but later Mehta put in the bureaucrat narrator as the 'sutradhaar' who becomes the 'sutra' or the thread who binds the stories round the 'dhar' or the river. In this novel she tries to bring mythological time, historical time, contemporary time and narrative time all together in the flow of the waters.

A River Sutra is a well chiseled narrative, a perfect work of art, unobtrusively bringing out the eternal human impulse behind all stories "to make sense of each moment by referring it to a larger narrative," says Bryan Appleyard of *The Sunday Times* and for this, he continues, "we need to live in a world not of our own making" (39). The novel tells a simple story about very basic ways of thinking about the world. But even the most simple stories are, according to Paul Cobley (2001, 2):

> "embedded in a network of relations that are sometimes astounding in their complexity [...] (Even) the most familiar, most primitive, most ancient and seemingly straightforward

of stories reveals depths that we might hitherto have failed to anticipate. That we do not anticipate is usually because we do not attend to the network of relations in which a story resides; but this is definitely not to say that we do not partake of these depths and the potential pleasure they yield."

The surface narrative, which is not the real narrative, is linear for one by one the narrator meets each of the characters, pilgrims who reveal one facet of 'history,' or 'truth.' The narrator is a 'Vanaprasthi' who has retired to the forest 'to reflect.' He admits that he "was simply not equipped to wander into the jungle and become a forest hermit, surviving on fruit and roots" (1). He chooses to take up a vacant post of a manager at a government rest house situated on the Narmada River as he had early in his touring career "developed an affection for these lonely scanturies built by the Moghul Emperors across the great expanse of India to shelter the traveller and the pilgrim" (2). The bungalow's proximity to the Narmada river was an added attraction since it was believed that the river's waters were purifying; even the sin of "attempted suicide is often ignored" if the offender is trying to kill himself in the sacred river's waters. He does not have to submerge himself into the river, but he does delve deep into the meaning of life by sharing varied lived experiences.

The first is of a Jain monk, a young man who has renounced the world like himself yet differently. For one the protagonist's renunciation becomes a consequential imperative, "my wife was barren so I had no children [...] my parents are no longer alive nor my wife, and my associates hardly noticed the moment of my departure" (12). But the monk's renunciation cost his father sixty-two million rupees and days of fanfare. Secondly, the protagonist had left more drastic lifestyles of the material world to reflect and the monk, in order not to inherit his father's inhumanity along with his business acumen; also the life of "unremitting pleasure ceased to satisfy me, leaving me exhausted from the last indulgence, while anticipating the next [...] I had already become fatigued with the world" (29). Now the monk roamed around with a begging bowl, though still remembering the doubts he had nurtured for this way of life, and unable to reveal anymore he departs to join his fellow monks at Mahadeo.

The next character story is of Master Mohan narrated by the protagonist's friend Jariq Mia. Mohan is a poor music teacher to whose custody fate brings a boy, young, blind, though, gifted with an astounding voice. A voice "only heard in dreams [...] such purity of tone was something that could be imagined, but never realised by the human voice" (61). Master Mohan's expertise so prunes this "voice of an angel" that the young boy soon gathers an audience and scores a record deal. However, here events take a sudden turn as the Master's wife (and children) who had always been complaining "waiting for him on the doorstep each day with fresh accusations about the blind boy's insolence, his clumsiness, his greed" (66), trades the boy to two sinister looking men watching Imrat daily for a large sum. To everyone's horror the boy's throat is slit as he is singing. And as we question why this happened, we are told through Jariq Mia, "Why does a man steal an object of worship so no one but himself can enjoy it" (90).

We move on then to meet a young aspiring business man, freshly learning the ways of the business world who is called on to manage an extremely remote tea plantation, away from the outside world. Severed from the main stream society he is used to, his sexual instincts lead him astray; this is only complicated by a visit from a friend who tells him, "it is downright sinister for a man [his] age not to have had a woman for two solid years!" (121). When studies and alcohol prove no reprieve, his co-workers send an anonymous women to his room to take care of his urges and he falls a victim to an awful "soul stealing" spell she casts on him. Suffering insanity for many days, the man hears of Narmada, the sacred healing spot and begins his journey.

At this point the cohesive force pulling the stories of these various travellers together becomes apparent. We realise that most of these characters, after attempting to do the right thing, end up being wronged in some way by the greediness inherent in modern society. And many of them, struck by insanity, visit the Narmada for cure. The similarity among them lies in their attempt to cast off the desire that drives men, and devote themselves to something, only to be disillusioned by the true ways of the world; Mr. Chagla says "the serpent in question is desire. Its venom is the harm a man does when he is ignoring the power of desire" (143).

The two final connections are made with the most important stories of the book. The protagonist, one day during a walk through the market place, meets a girl, the daughter of a master musician, pursuing her studies under her father. She recalls how her father would, during the two initial years of her training, not let her touch an instrument, but make her sit out in the woods searching for the notes of the scale in nature. She eventually becomes a master in her craft and is "married," in a ceremony, to the God of music. This story impresses upon the reader that nature has a stronger, a deeper and an everlasting impact than men. It was said earlier in the book, "men are fools, they think only humans respond to beauty. But a geeing deer will drop its food to listen to music, and a king cobra sway its hood in pleasure" (204). It stands quite evident that man has wandered out of nature, ignored its true power and thus, marred his chances for being at one and at peace with it.

The last actor in the drama is a river minstrel (a holy ascetic hermit, who wanders around like a monk, worshipping and chanting to the river), who saves a young girl from a brothel and with her moves into the forest, away from the society. After several years, the minstrel, Naga Baba, abandons this girl who was "more than a child to him" and sets off "to find the next stage of enlightenment" (258).

As the book reaches its climax, we are shown the main character playing host to a team of archeologists headed by a Professor Shankar. A discussion over the Narmada reveals what varied aspects it can have—mystical for the protagonist and merely historical for the realistic professor. The professor claims he loves the river, "but worship is too strong a word [...] I am a man and understand only other men" (271).

At the behest of the protagonist, a river minstrel is called for to illuminate him on the holiness of the river. To his and the readers' shock this river minstrel is Uma, the young girl Naga Baba had raised and Professor Shankar is none other than the

Naga Baba himself. To the protagonist's "he is in a cave somewhere seeking higher enlightenment" (281), we hear, "No. He has re-entered the world."

This indeed is continuity, another form of immortality—the true recognition of life. "What we are seeing today is the same river that was seen by the people who lived here a hundred thousand years ego. To me such a sustained record of human presence in the same place—that is immortality" (264).

The river thus, in its historic and mythic presence becomes an archetype of fertility and immortality. Nineteen kilometers away is the town of Rudra, (named after the angry incarnation of Lord Shiva), and at the bend of the river, sprawls the temple complex of Mahadeo (the name of the deity himself). There lies a tribal village nearby by the name of Vano, or forest, which is inhabited by the descendants of the races that held the Aryan invasion of India at bay for centuries. The Vano village deity "cures madness, liberating those who are possessed" (6).

The source of the river is at the Amarkantak (the seat of immortality) and the pilgrims that traverse that path, through their endurance, "hope to generate the heat, the tapas, that links men to the energy of the universe, as the Narmada River is thought to link mankind to the energy of Shiva" (8).

"It is said that Shiva, Creator and Destroyer of Worlds, was in an ascetic trance so strenuous that rivulets of perspiration began flowing from his body down the hills. The stream took on the form of a woman—the most dangerous of her kind: a beautiful virgin innocently tempting even ascetics to pursue her, inflaming their lust by appearing at one moment as a lightly dancing girl, at another as a romantic dreamer, at yet another as a seductress loose limbed with the lassitude of desire. Her inventive variations so amused Shiva that he named her Narmada, the Delightful One, blessing her with the words "You shall be forever holy, forever inexhaustible." Then he gave her in marriage to the ocean, Lord of Rivers, most lustrous of all her suitors" (8-9).

Thus, a linear narrative, a simple story gathers into its fold entangled threads of representation. Along with the flow of the river, the stories movement acquires a captivating potential as it involves in its trail diversions, detours and digressions. The movement towards disclosure, its linear dynamics, thus becomes an equivalent of the poetic effect of metonymy the sequential linking of events according to their common association in part or whole. The digressions also reflect upon the diversity of Hinduism. "Indians," says Tariq Mia, "have never been prepared to settle for a single mythology if they could squeeze a hundred in" (145).

This novel, a string of bio-sketches, creates a sense of interconnectedness as it examines the possibilities and impossibilities of living an Indian life according to the 'Dharma' or 'Truth' of the Hindu religion. This right path, established in the Mahabharata, seems to have become something almost unattainable given today's culture. As the various main characters of this book come to prove, the stark contrasts between living the supremely holy life, like that of the monks, and a normal everyday life, in a corrupted society make combining the two impossible. In this way the subplots that reveal the underlying mysticism become the real narrative of the novel through which the narrator 'meets' life, not retires from it.

WORKS CITED

Appleyard, Bryan, *Sunday Times Magazine*, February 1999.

Cobley, Paul, *Narrative*, London: Routledge, 2001.

Mehta, Gita, *A River Sutra*, New Delhi: Penguin Books, 1993 (All references and page numbers are from this edition).

22

Culture Commodification and the Market: Bharati Mukherjee's Fiction Diasporic Writer

NAFISA HATMI

In the contemporary inter/intra cultural space the role of a writer as a negotiator or that of a mediator is debatable. Still, a properly focused 'gaze' is quite capable of decoding the obliquely camouflaged stance a particular writer adopts in his/her work to enhance the marketability of the product. As Surveyor of remote "culture," the writer strategically locates their works as the only appropriate alternative/medium for an intra/inter cultural dialogue or may be trade off. The paper is an attempt to analyse the novels of Bharati Mukherjee (*Wife, Jasmine & The Holder of the World*), along the above stated lines.

Bharati Mukherjee's fiction emerges as a text loaded with a 'Cultural Cargo' heading or targeted at a specific, *i.e.,* Western market/audience. Her textural strategies of collecting, cataloguing and packaging become evident once the veil of high-literaryness is lifted and the hidden agenda is exposed through close reading. There are of course degrees of variability in terms of 'cultural loading'—may be according to necessary modulations in relation to the trade environment—her major novels betray a remarkable consistency, which may raise a few eyebrows and may in turn become highly objectionable. This apparent commodification of culture while it is an apparent loss and demeaning for the native, acts as a counter valence for her art as a whole and reduces it to the category of 'non-art.'

For the purpose of theoretical reference, the paper borrows

its argumentative vigour from James Clifford's essay "On Collecting Art & Culture" from Simon During's edited anthology on *The Cultural Studies.*

> Since the turn of the century objects collected from non-Western sources have been classified in two major categories: as (scientific) cultural artifacts or as (aesthetic) works of art. Other collectables—mass-produced commodities, 'tourist art,' curios, and so on—have been less systematically valued; at best they find a place in exhibits of 'technology' or 'folklore.' These and other locations within what may be called the 'modern art-culture system' can be visualised with the help of a (somewhat procrustean) diagram.
>
> A.J. Greimas's 'semiotic square' (Gremas and Rustier 1968) shows us 'that any initial binary opposition can, by the operation of negations and the appropriate synthesis, generate a much larger field of terms which, however, all necessarily remain locked in the closure of the initial system' (Jameson 1981: 62). Adapting Greimas for the purposes of cultural criticism, Fredric Jameson uses the semiotic square to reveal 'the limits of a specific ideological consciousness, (marketing) the conceptual points beyond which that consciousness cannot go, and between which it is condemned to oscillate' (1981: 47). Following his example, I offer the following map (see diagram) of a historically specific, contestable field of meanings and institutions.
>
> Beginning with an initial opposition, by a process of negation four terms are generated. This establishes horizontal and vertical axes and between them four semantic zones: (1) the zone of authentic masterpieces, (2) the zone of authentic artifacts, (3) the zone of in-authentic masterpieces, (4) the zone of in-authentic artifacts. Most objects—old and new, rare and common, familiar and exotic—can be located in one of these zones or ambiguously, in traffic, between two zones.
>
> The system classifies objects and assigns them relative value. It establishes the 'contexts' in which they properly

belong and between which they circulate. Regular movements towards positive value proceed from bottom to top and from right to left. These movements select artifacts of enduring worth or rarity, their value normally guaranteed by a 'vanishing' cultural status or by the selection and pricing mechanisms of the art market. The value of Shaker crafts reflects the fact that Shaker society no longer exists: the stock is limited. In the art world work is recognised as 'important' by connoisseurs and collectors according to criteria that are more than simply aesthetic (see Becker 1982). Indeed, prevailing definitions of what is 'beautiful' or 'interesting' sometimes change quite rapidly.

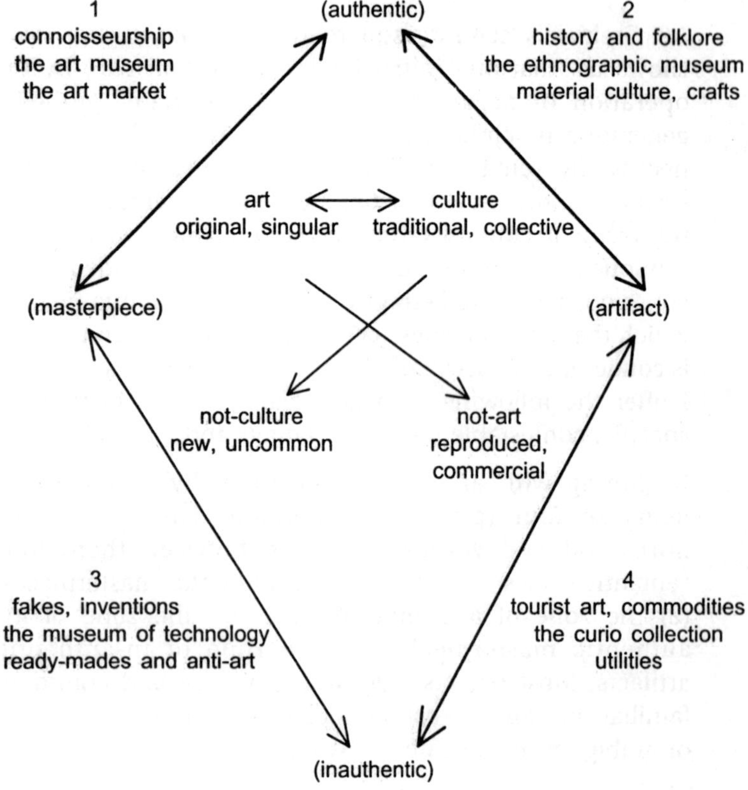

> The semiotic square indicates that through selection and pricing mechanism of the art market there is a regular movement in which positive values move from inauthentic to authentic art. The movement that is revealed in the novels of Bharati Mukherjee is in inverse direction as she contextualizes the Indian culture and history in order to create a space for acceptance so as to enable her to market her art. The commodification of culture is evident in the progress of her heroines who come to America 'greedy with wants and reckless with hope' and have a firm belief that their dreams would be realised in the promised land.

Bharati Mukherjee is an Indian immigrant in Canada and she writes in her introduction to the collection of short stories that her transformation as a writer occurred with the act of immigration. In her novels we find "a movement away from the aloofness of expatriation, to the exuberance of immigration." Her 'immigration' story is replicated in the heroines of her novels who "greedy with wants and reckless with hope" choose America as the land where their dreams would be realised. Indianness in a mere metaphor used either ironically or nostalgically or as an asset to act as a counter valence for her art.

In her early novel *Wife* (1975) the heroine Dimple challenges the traditional concept of Indian wife and womanhood. She succeeds in subverting her Bengali upbringing by migrating to America. With ease she identifies herself with American consumer culture. The T.V. adds, magazines help her to Americanise herself. The first thing that awes Dimple in America are the skyscrapers and enormous cars speeding in lanes. She is thrilled with bigness. She dreams of a large apartment at Queens, with a large queen size beds, big leather chairs and lamps, contextualisation in the terms of consumer culture to a large extent substitutes her Bengali upbringing. Her attitude towards her husband Amit changes accordingly. The Sita myth is subverted and Bharati Mukherjee laughs at the myth when she describes Sita in the wall-hanging at the Sen's apartment—"a short, voluptuous Sita hip-deep in pale orange flames." In bitter moments Dimple ranks "husband, blender, colour T.V. cassette, tape recorder, stereo in their order of convenience."

Bharati Mukherjee makes Dimple stride through the golden moments of consumer society, but the twin adversity of her still being the 'wife' and the subverting horror of a thoroughly evolved capitalist social system overwhelms even her fantasies. The whole momentum of the text whimpers down to the blurred images of TV screen and dream fading in and out. New York city fails to materialize into the forest of Aden and Dimple Basu is not imbrued with enough Rosailindesque resoluteness. Ironically, Dimple is not even a wife, but reduced to a waiving waif and therefore the novel ends thus "women on television got away with murder."

The cross-cultural metamorphosis in her next novel *Jasmine* (1989) presents a facade of Indianisation and Bharati Mukherjee who is aware of the fact that she cannot do away with her Indian label, overts her anti-Indian stance, which is quite blatant in *Wife*. In *Jasmine*, she writes about the "Small Trade off between new world reasonableness and old-world beliefs." She presents the fluid and fragile identity of the protagonist who progresses from Jyoti to Jasmine and then to Jessie and finally Jane in a short span of six years.

Unlike Dimple, Jasmine believes in her marriage vows and keeps the memory of her dead husband alive and makes it her strength. She decides to go to America to pursue her husband's dream of opening their own store "Vijh & Wife." After his death she refuses to be the part of the feudal order of Hansapur—'Jyoti is dead' and Jasmine reaches America. Her odyssey through America is caught up with violence. She arrives in America along with outcastes, deporters, strange pilgrims, dressed in their national costumes who appear as "wilted plumage of intercontinental vagabondage." She had a long way to go before she could achieve her mission—to reach the place in the photograph Prakash dreamed of reaching, burn his suit along with paper and twigs and throw herself into the fire in her white saree. She carries the sandalwood Ganapati—a god with an elephant trunk to uproot anything that came in her path. It gives her strength to fight the advances of a half-faced men and save her honour by murdering him. Bharati Mukherjee pictures Jasmine as Kali. In *Wife* she mocks at the Sita image whereas in this novel Bharati Mukherjee shows mock respect when she describes the urge of Jasmine to perform Sati in America when it is no longer prevalent in India. The novelist's intentions are quite clear for in the course of the novel Jasmine makes no such attempt. In the process of adapting herself in America she leaves Hansapur behind and ironically tries to create Hansapur in America itself. Planting culture is something that is not possible and the novelist's attempt to do so is a strategy to locate her work.

Dimple arrives in America and is soon confronted with skyscrappers and endless lines of cars whereas Jasmine carries India within her and seeks familiarity in the fields and the crops and feels "she has never left India." She stays with three families, first with Professor Dave Vadhera—the esteemed teacher of her husband. She is shocked to learn the reality of Professor's reality in America and seeks shelter and help from the daughter of Mrs. Gordan. Kate introduces her to Taylor household and she stays with them to look after their little daughter. Jasmine is happy with her new role of caretaker and showers all her love and care on all members of the family. She takes various courses and through her training earns extra money. Taylor is attracted towards her and gradually Willie and Taylor drift apart. Taylor wants Jasmine to become his Jessie and she almost agrees to become a member of his family. A chance encounter with the murderer of her husband sends her rushing to Iowa where she stays with Bud. Bud divorces his wife. He is a banker and one day just like Prakash is shot. His life is saved but he loses his legs and becomes invalid. Bud calls her Jane and she devotes herself nursing him and making his life happy. But in reality as Bud's wife points out that she brings trouble wherever she goes. In India an astrologer fortells her widowhood and exile and his prophecy is echoed in Karin's words who regards her as a "tornado, rubble-maker, arising from nowhere and disappearing into a cloud."

Bharati Mukherjee's culture collecting and plunging reaches its climax in her latest novel *The Holder of the World*. It is becoming more and more refined and the marketing is more consumer savvy and updated and takes into account the refinement and progress made in global trade, incorporating computer software and technology. The novel opens with the wonders possible through communication breakways. It will enable Beigh Masters a young American woman to "live in three time zones simultaneously." Her friend Venn Iyer establishes a grid a database which will enable them to work on interaction with a personality.

Beigh Masters assumes the role of 'culture purveyor' and is out to recreate the history of Hunnah 'the Salem Bibi' belonging to the Seventeenth Century. She visits the Museum of Maritime Art and is fascinated with the paintings of Hannah. She learns about the existence of a diamond known as "the Emperor's tear" and as an asset hunter undertakes a journey to India in order to discover the story behind the gem. The paintings in the museum though interesting are passive and indifferent. However, they are an active testimony of a living moment and Beigh Masters with the help of computer technology wants to cross culture and time so that she can place her data in its original and authentic cultural context.

Bharati Mukherjee changes the ground of her tale. The novel is not the story of an Indian immigrant to America struggling to establish identity in the dream country. It is the story of the encounter between two American women belonging to different centuries in India. Bharati Mukherjee describes India as a magic land and the two women are wrapped up in its spell. The novelist successfully turns the tale as an asset which she uses to find value and space in the literary market and prove herself as one of the foremost American writers.

The novelist's literary skills, her remarkable art of story-telling, her clarity, tenderness and humour makes her a good writer but the question raised and answered in my paper is why is a work saleable?

To sell her product Bharati Mukherjee packages her work by using superficial myths and tradition and distorting her own cultural values. She mocks at the traditional values and suggests American consumer culture is a better alternative and therefore even though her novels deal with the struggle of immigrants they also celebrate their success in the dreamland. Young Indians aspiring to immigrate find her novels as an answer to their doubts. If a middle-class Bengali girl and a village simpleton like Jasmine can Americanise themselves why cannot they and naturally her novels find market in India and in the West too. Thus, Bharati Mukherjee succeeds in her role as mediator between the two countries.

List of Contributors

S.C. Singh, retd. Associate Professor, former Head, Department of English, University of Rajasthan, Jaipur.

Ratri Ray, Professor, Department of English, Patna University, Patna.

Sangita Nagpal, Lecturer, Department of English, Subodh Girls College, Jaipur.

Arun Soule, Assistant Professor, Department of English, University of Rajasthan, Jaipur.

Suman Mehta, Lecturer, Department of English, Madhavanand Girls College, Bani Park, Jaipur.

K.V. Surendran, Lecturer, Institute of English and Foreign Languages, Kannur University, Kannur, Kerala.

Joya Chakravarty, Associate Professor, Department of English, University of Rajasthan, Jaipur.

Nishi Upadhyaya, Lecturer, Govt. P.G. College, Dausa, Rajasthan.

Suresh Shukla, retd. Professor of English, H.K. College of Commerce, Ahmedabad.

Namratha Mogaral, Lecturer, Department of English, Kuvempu University, Shimoga, Karnataka.

Nandini Nayar, Research Associate, Department of English, Kavempu University, Shimoga, Karnataka.

Pramod K. Nayar, Assistant Professor, Department of English, University of Hyderabad, Hyderabad.

Jaydipsinh Dodiya, Lecturer, Department of English, Saurashtra University, Rajkot.

Ashok K. Tiwari, Associate Professor, Department of English, University of Rajasthan, Jaipur.

Ravi Nandan Sinha, Associate Professor, Deptt. of English, St. Xavier's College, Ranchi.

Nafisa Hatmi, Head Department of English, M.L. Sukhadia University, Udaipur, Rajasthan.

Vandana Sharma, Lecturer in English, Poornima College of Engineering, Sitapura, Jaipur.

Indira Nityanandam, Lecturer in English, Navgujarat Arts College, Ahmedabad.

Poonam Yadav, Research Scholar, Department of English, University of Rajasthan, Jaipur.

Shubhshree, Research Scholar, Department of English, University of Rajashtan, Jaipur.